MISSISSIPPI IN TRANSITION:

THE ROLE OF THE MISSISSIPPI HUMANITIES COUNCIL

CORA NORMAN

Edited by Judy Elgin

TENNESSEE VALLEY

Publishing®

2009

Library of Congress Control Number: 2009926393

Published by:
    Tennessee Valley Publishing
    PO Box 52527
    Knoxville, Tennessee 37950-2527
    info@tvp1.com

Printed and bound in the United States of America.

ISBN-13: 978-1-932604-69-6
ISBN-10: 1-932604-69-3

DEDICATION

Following my retirement after twenty-four years of service with the council, it took years to put this book together. I dedicated it to Mother and Daddy, who believed that I could do anything, giving me self confidence; to Bob and Judy, who gave me immortality; and to Katharine Rea, my mentor, travel companion and everlasting friend.

I remain very close to my son and daughter. Both worked hard in preparation for their careers and through the years demonstrated their commitment, intellect, and concern for people. Bob, a former Marine officer, is in his 21st year as prosecutor in the U.S. Attorney's Office in the Northern District of Mississippi. Judy received her nurse practitioner degree and worked for the Veterans Administration for nine years. She is now into holistic medicine with her own Elgin Center in Crossville, Tennessee.

I wrote about my relationship with Katharine Rea as one of my "Agents of Change in Mississippi during the Twentieth Century." Katharine knew her students, and I was no exception. When I lost my father in 1971 during graduate work, Katharine knew my pain. She handed me a book to read, saying, "You need a good cry."

I want to thank all who took the time to read my work and make helpful comments: Lara McCaulley, Phil Elgin, Peggy Prenshaw, Jane Crater Hiatt, Gemma Beckley and Bill Parrish. I owe Brenda Gray for so much during our years

iii

together and for constantly digging out information for this book. I am deeply indebted to my daughter Judy Elgin for taking the time from her professional work to edit my writing. She taught me a lot about writing!

TABLE OF CONTENTS

PREFACE
WHY I WROTE THE BOOK

I wanted to write about the founding of the Mississippi Committee for the Humanities, the people who were involved, the challenges and the obstacles they encountered. In 2005 I spent several months going through all my files deposited at the Mississippi Department of Archives and History. A copy of every letter I wrote and all letters received while I was with the Mississippi Humanities Council are filed with Archives and History. At the 2007 MHC Awards Banquet with almost 400 attending, I felt anew the urge to write the early story.

We started with a very committed council, and by 2007 a federal judge, a congressman, members of the Mississippi legislature, academicians from every college and university in the state, state-wide leaders, Chairman of the National Endowment of the Humanities Bruce Cole, and Carol Watson with NEH attended the awards banquet. In the early years, if we claimed an audience of 40 persons we were elated.

I chose not to focus on specific programs funded by the council but instead to focus on persons involved because all were willing to support programs open to all citizens of the state—not a popular idea in Mississippi in the early days. Through the years, the programs addressed a wide variety of issues concerning education, women's rights, agriculture, the U. S. Constitution, justice, work, multiculturalism, urbanization, land use, politics, and health.

In 1987 the name changed from Mississippi Committee for the Humanities (MCH) to Mississippi Humanities Council (MHC). The same logo, designed by Sally Vaughan at the University of Mississippi for our first stationery, continued to be used with the rearrangement of the letters. In writing the book, I decided that using both names would be very confusing to the readers, so, except in direct quotes, I used Mississippi Humanities Council (MHC) throughout.

The names of five of our colleges changed to include "university" in one day during Governor Waller's tenure. Likewise, all junior colleges except Jones Junior College changed to community colleges. Therefore, I referred to the institutions of higher learning by their current names.

My Background and Personal Introduction To Civil Rights

Looking at my background, I realized how blessed I was to be born into my family of origin. I was the only child and knew I was loved. I knew that I was my daddy's favorite and that he would always work that I might have more than he had. My mother was from a very loving family, and it was her family that gave me my foundation for appreciation for the work of others.

We lived in a rural area in Columbia County, Arkansas. Funds were very limited, but food was always plentiful in our home and was shared with those who did not have as much as we had. My father had a monthly paycheck from Mobil Oil Company and eventually got two of my mother's brothers on their payroll. The rest of the family depended upon the land for what they had.

Even though my family practiced segregation—the status was accepted and never questioned—they also showed me that friendships crossed racial lines. Some of my earliest caregivers were black women.

I grew up when few of the adults finished high school and not one of them went to college. However, they valued education and the contributions of the church. My maternal grandfather was known in his community for building churches and a school. My daddy, an oil field worker, never questioned my interest in seeking an education. He was always there with a helping hand. When I graduated from Magnolia Agricultural & Mechanical College, now University of Southern Arkansas in Magnolia, with an associate's degree, my father and mother were there, as was my grandfather Beasley.

When I started college, my goals were to attend medical school, become a doctor, and help others. It was during my second year of college that I met Bill Norman, who taught at Magnolia A & M College. I had organic chemistry, analytical chemistry, and physics under him, and by the end of the first semester, I knew that he had an interest in me. I never dated, and with a professor pursuing me, I was overwhelmed by his attention. Looking back, I realized that I was doomed!

After graduating from Magnolia A & M, I spent the summer in Fayetteville at the University of Arkansas continuing my education while awaiting acceptance to the University of Arkansas Medical School in Little Rock. Bill visited me several times that summer and insisted that I not pursue a medical career. However, I enrolled that fall. It was at the end of World War II, and most of the freshman class at the medical school was made up of army recruits. There were about one hundred students, and only three or four were female. There were no dormitories at the medical school, and although nearby private homes rented rooms to the males, they didn't want any females since females always left their wet underwear in the bathrooms. Another female student and I finally rented a large room that was originally offered to four working women but was many blocks away from the school. I was well aware that the cost of my staying there would be a great burden for my mother and daddy, yet neither ever mentioned the cost factor to me.

Just prior to the end of my first semester, I contracted pneumonia and missed my final exams. Then another event occurred—one of a different nature that more dramatically interrupted my pursuit of a medical degree.

Bill drove me back to Little Rock after the Christmas holidays and on the way professed his love for me. I soon found that my roommate moved out over Christmas and left me with a room and rent all to myself. Faced with make-up exams, no roommate, and Bill insisting we marry, I submitted to hormones; I quit. My exit interview with the dean of the medical college was memorable. He told me that I took a space a man might have had and who, no doubt, would have survived and become a doctor.

Cora and Bill Norman—60 Years Later. . .

Bill and I married in 1946 and went directly to El Paso, Texas, where he had a position in the chemistry department at what was then the College of Mines and Metallurgy and is now the University of Texas at El Paso. Without any objections from Bill, I immediately enrolled to complete my bachelor's degree. It was immediately after the close of World War II, and the classes were full of married male veterans. I was the only married female pursuing a degree in chemistry. One of my classmates asked if I intended to raise my baby in a test tube in the laboratory. After our first child, our son, was born, I finished my course work and received a bachelor's degree in chemistry. My graduating class was the first to finish under the college's new name, Texas Western College.

Bill promised that he would return to school to work toward a Ph.D., and I kept hoping that there would be a medical school nearby so that I could pursue my dream. After four years in El Paso, we had no money saved, so I got a job with El Paso Natural Gas Company. I was the first faculty wife to take a job off campus. After one year we saved $2,000 and moved to the University of Texas in Austin for Bill to return to graduate school. It was a long and arduous stint while Bill worked on his degree.

Like so many other women of my generation, I redirected my ambition to the support of a husband. I first worked in the Auditor's Office at the University of Texas and then went to the Internal Revenue Service because the pay was a little better. I became pregnant and worked until just a few weeks before giving birth to our daughter. I asked for maternity leave, which they denied. I even carried my appeal to the top executive, who still denied it. I began to type dissertations at home to pay the bills. We would never have made it if my parents had not helped us so much. My parents had a country store at the time, and almost daily I received a letter with cash from my mother. After our second child was born, Daddy even presented us with a new car. Bill finished his course work, and I earned a P.H.T.S. (Putting Hubby through School). The president of the university signed the certificate and presented it to me.

With all course work finally completed, Bill took a job at the University of South Carolina while working on his dissertation. After years of living on my meager income, I loved my life in Columbia and chose to not work for the first two years. I dealt with the bills while Bill was in graduate school but announced after the move that he would pay all future bills. I joined a women's club and the faculty club and was active in the Methodist church. You might imagine my chagrin, after living in Columbia for only one month, when the neighborhood awakened one morning to the utility company cutting off our water supply because Bill forgot to pay the water bill! I again took over the task that has continued throughout our marriage.

When Bill received his Ph.D. from the University of Texas, he began looking for a permanent job. His two job offers came from a school in northern New York, almost on the Canadian border, and the Department of Biology at the University of Mississippi. We chose the University of Mississippi because it was closer to our extended family, but it was a difficult and reluctant choice because of the emerging civil rights movement. Bill, a Texan, and I, an Arkansan, were very much aware of the struggles in the South in the early 1960s, and we were integrationists in principle. But our beliefs conflicted with those of our family and friends and were never discussed. We feared isolation from our loved ones if we made a public stand so wanted no active part in the civil rights movement.

Looking back, I realized the great disparity between the perspectives of educated and uneducated individuals. Bill and I had the opportunity to discuss issues with others within the classroom setting and were probably much more open to different belief systems. We were not only open to controversial discussions but encouraged them and did so throughout the years raising our children. We continue to do so.

However, extended family and friends, born and raised in the traditional South, accepted the segregationist practices without question. My love and respect for them prevented open discussions. I felt an internal conflict for years following our move to Mississippi. As stated earlier, I received tremendous love and acceptance from my extended family throughout my lifetime, and I felt I put that in jeopardy if I brought up the issue of integration with them.

It was 1971 when I finally broached the subject with my father while informing him that my daughter had a black female roommate at Southwestern at Memphis. When Judy registered as a freshman, she had the option of choosing a black roommate and did so. Although I anticipated Daddy would go into a rage because he adored his granddaughter, his reaction surprised me. He was completely silent for several minutes and then merely said, "Times are changing." I still had not told my mother. Following my father's death in the fall of 1971, she and I were on the campus to visit when Mother discovered the black roommate. There was no reaction while in the dorm room, but back in the car she simply said, "Why didn't you tell me?"

We arrived in Oxford, Mississippi, in 1961 and found it to be a very segregated society. Our lessons in civil rights began almost immediately. Since I worked full-time, we hired our first housekeeper, Minnie. She also cared for our children Bob and Judy, who were in eighth and second grades.

We planned a trip to Greenville, Mississippi, to meet my mother, Bob and Judy, and a new member of the extended family, Linda Wreyford. We invited Minnie to go with us as she had never been outside the Oxford area. She accepted and prepared a traditional southern picnic lunch of barbequed chicken, potato salad, and baked beans for us to carry with us. Just before arriving in Greenville, I overturned our Ford Falcon. The local ambulance transported Bill, Minnie, and me to the local hospital. We were covered in barbeque sauce, beans, and salad. Bill had minor injuries and was ambulatory, but Minnie and I had more serious injuries. We refused admission to the hospital because we knew Minnie would be segregated from us. There was only one examination table in the emergency room, so Minnie and I took turns lying on the table. We did that all afternoon until we got into Mother's car for the drive back to Oxford. Minnie needed to see her doctor the next morning per medical instruction. I insisted on going with her, even into the segregated waiting room where the blacks stared at me, but I was determined to stay with Minnie.

Our lessons, and eventual participation, in the civil rights movement continued during the fall of 1962 when James Meredith, the first black student at a southern university, integrated Ole Miss. We were building a house near the campus and planned to move into it later that fall. On Sunday afternoon, September 30, we planned to clean the brick fireplace in the new house and needed acid from Bill's lab to finish the task. While on campus we witnessed the arrival of the first load of federal marshals. They encircled the Lyceum (administration) building prior to Meredith's admittance. Realizing the importance of the moment, Bill ran into his office, grabbed his camera, and took the following pictures of the troops arriving in front of the Lyceum Building.

For weeks prior to this incident, members of the press and citizens from around the state who opposed Meredith's arrival invaded the campus. That night, with federal marshals and more than 20,000 troops standing guard, the riot erupted, killing two people.

We lived several blocks from Oxford's town square at that time, and troops were everywhere. We had a patrol camped in our front yard. The morning after their arrival we made a big pot of coffee, and my husband took it out to share with the troops. Not one soldier took a cup of coffee—they thought it might be poisoned!

I worked on campus in Continuing Education with Conferences and Institutes, housed in the Continuation Center. When two white federal marshals finally escorted James Meredith to the university, they brought him to the Continuation Center to register for admittance. Governor Ross Barnett came to the campus to personally admit him. We already had more than 20,000 troops in the Oxford area to ensure Meredith's arrival was peaceful. The administrators moved from the administration offices in the Lyceum to the Continuation Center to escape the media on campus. They pulled the drapes and told the secretarial staff to go home. When two of us asked if we could stay, they told us we could if we were very quiet; we stayed. Governor Barnett went into the office of Bill Jones, director of Conferences and Institutes, to talk to U. S. Attorney General Bobby Kennedy over the telephone. The governor's side of the conversation was very polite. When Meredith and the marshals approached him, Barnett asked, "Which one of you is Meredith?"

Faced with a mortgage and the real possibility that Ole Miss would lose its accreditation with the admittance of a black student, we feared we made a terrible choice in moving to Oxford. The professors in the chemistry department left en masse.

The months following Meredith's admission found many changes in community life at Ole Miss and in Oxford. The segregationists immediately separated from the integrationists, as well as the town from the campus. I joined the League of Women Voters in 1961, but after this incident, all the women from Oxford withdrew their membership, leaving only University women as members.

We joined the local Human Relations Council. Such groups sprang up throughout the state to offer some semblance of sanity in our communities. At the University of Mississippi, Dr. Katharine Rea and a few other professors offered sensitivity training for those southerners like myself who previously never questioned why we practiced segregation. During the early 1960s, Katharine invited a black woman from New York to the campus and arranged a luncheon at the university cafeteria for a small group to meet with her. Katharine made sure that I sat next to the woman at lunch. I had never eaten a meal with a black person prior to that time. Looking back, it all seemed so insane when we believed that God is Father to us all.

I began to think more about the practices taught in the South. Everything was segregated. On the grounds of the Oxford courthouse there were separate rest rooms and a separate water fountain labeled "For Colored." Because of our circumstances, our views were different, and it was obvious that we were integrationists. Our beliefs forced us to take a public stand.

My parents brought me up in the church, and we attended church services regularly. My husband and I were both members of the Board of Stewards of the Methodist Church, and I was the so-called head of Social Concerns. At a meeting of the stewards (not the entire church membership), I suggested that we meet with our counterparts in the black Methodist church. You would have thought that I had already invited the blacks to our church. Without any discussion, the board gave the thumbs down to my suggestion, and the atmosphere in the room immediately chilled. I left the meeting and said that was enough. I always attended church and knew that if I missed a Sunday there would be telephone calls, but I never received a call. Several years later one of the men at that church simply said, "We miss you, Cora." This scenario could have transpired in any white church in Mississippi during that time; I now look for ecumenical services.

Before that event though, we had a mature Turkish woman Mrs. Arkun working on a master's degree in the sciences at the University of Mississippi. She lived in student housing, and I often took her grocery shopping. After several months, her husband came to the States to stay with her, having recently retired from his work in Turkey. They went with us to the Methodist church one Sunday when we observed Communion Sunday. Mr. Arkun asked me if he could take communion with us. Even though he was Muslim, I was not about to tell him, "No." If the members of that church had known, I might have been forced to leave the church earlier that I did! It seemed that our churches were the very last to desegregate.

It was the mid-1960s before we had the first black graduate student in the biology department—George Williams, who worked on his master's degree under my husband. George frequented our home, and there were times he opened up and shared with us incidents of discrimination he endured on campus. He survived and received his degree. George became a life-long friend and continues to call regularly to check on my husband.

It was stressful during the sixties. When we attended mixed groups, we usually saw a carload of white men outside taking names of all those attending. Yet we had enough friends who felt as we did, and we bonded more closely with them as we welcomed the few blacks into our group. The League of Women Voters' first black members were Della Davidson and a woman with my name, Cora.

When schools desegregated in 1969-70, the communities throughout the state faced immediate problems, and our school superintendents found themselves in the middle of the chaos. What were truly community issues became problems for the superintendents to address and solve. Schools had to be consolidated, but how were they to accomplish that feat? There were many questions: How to decide which school campuses to use or which school name, colors, or mascot; how to promote communication between blacks and whites, teachers and students, parents and teachers; how to discipline the students of another race without creating further problems. Some superintendents suffered medical crises from the increased stress, and some retired early. In promoting humanities programs for all citizens to discuss public policy issues, I found that the superintendents had no interest in opening schools at night for integrated meetings.

Looking back, with all the tribulations, it was not possible to have a life more rewarding than those thirty-five years following Meredith's entrance to the University of Mississippi. I became involved in the civil rights movement, the women's movement, and the fight to keep our public schools open. Our dinner table became the place where we discussed the activities of the day with our children, and race relations were always a topic. We entertained our foreign students, and thus began my interest in intercultural activities.

Due to the efforts of Dr. Katharine Rea, I received an American Association of University Women (AAUW) scholarship in 1963 to begin work on my master's degree in chemistry. It was a pilot program targeting southeastern women to discover if we had the sense to do graduate work after being out of school with a bachelor's degree for a minimum of fifteen years! There were only two from Mississippi to receive such a scholarship—myself and Kate Wilkerson. With my money, I bought a dish washer. At one point I had trouble in my analytical chemistry class, and my professor said, "That's a hell of a way to pay for a dishwasher." However, I received my master's degree in chemistry from the University of Mississippi.

Bill became involved with the National Science Foundation, directed institutes at Ole Miss, and later served a year at the NSF offices in Washington, D. C. Perhaps by often helping Bill with the budgets he submitted to NSF, I laid the foundation for my future work with the MHC. His first institute in 1970 for teachers of state community colleges brought both black and white teachers to Ole Miss. In fact, the co-chair of the first institute was Frank Gambrell, dean from Coahoma Community College (a predominately black college at that time). That summer, Dean Gambrell's wife worked on a master's degree in home economics at Ole Miss. They had a daughter about the same age as ours, and we invited the daughter to spend a week at our house before the end of the summer workshop.

Bill and I planned a reception to be held at our home for the institute persons, and there was much discussion at the dinner table about opening our home to a mixed group. Our daughter listened, and when we announced the get-together, Judy asked if she could invite her new-found friend from high school—a black boy. We knew nothing about this attraction and were dumbfounded! "Absolutely not!" was our answer. Our son Bob was in the U. S. Marines, and Judy wrote her brother that we were not as open and liberal as we seemed with our friends! I included this story because it shows what we faced, but the story continued. I immediately refrained from pursuing the invitation for the Gambrell's daughter to spend a week with us at our home. Several months later, I tried to explain to Mrs. Gambrell what happened in our household. She laughed and told her story. About that same time, their daughter was at Alcorn State University and met a white boy to whom she was very much attracted. When Dean Gambrell heard of his daughter's attraction, he took his gun and went to Alcorn to stop that relationship! Needless to say, it was not an unusual story of the times.

After receiving my master's degree, I taught science at Holly Springs High School and the following year taught chemistry and biology at the newly built Lafayette County High School. I then returned to the Continuation Center to be administrative assistant to Director Maurice Inman. My desk was in his office, and I drafted all his correspondence. During that time I had my introduction to community colleges and to statewide programs in Mississippi.

I never gave up my goal of graduate study and in the late 1960s began working on my doctoral program, taking one course per semester. In early 1972 my life turned in a new and unexpected direction. The previous year my father died from lung cancer, and my mother came to Mississippi from Arkansas to help as I finished my final degree requirements. Bill was still in the Biology Department at Ole Miss, and we had two adult children—Bob, a captain in the Marine Corps, and Judy, a freshman at what is now Rhodes College in

Memphis, Tennessee. Just after completing the course work and final examinations for my degree, I received a telephone call from Dr. Thomas Flynn, professor of philosophy at the University of Mississippi; he offered me the position of staff administrator for the new state-based humanities program. That call changed my career plans and turned me in a new and exciting direction.

I knew of Dr. Flynn—my son Bob took a philosophy course under him—but he certainly knew nothing of me. He took on the job of finding a staff person for the new Mississippi Humanities Council. It was after retiring twenty-four years later that I discovered Tom Flynn talked with my friend, Katharine Rea, prior to his telephoning me. Katharine really landed me the job with the humanities program. She was well respected on campus and apparently recommended me without reservation; Tom Flynn accepted whatever she said. I met Katharine through the American Association of University Women when we first moved to Oxford in 1961. At that time she was dean of women at the University. Later she became professor of higher education. She was not my major professor, but we became very good friends, and she was certainly my counselor. However, if I had known what was expected of me, I am sure I would have refused the job. I had no background in the humanities. Yet one's destiny is sometimes foreordained.

I wished I had a videotape of Tom Flynn's meeting with Porter Fortune, chancellor of the University of Mississippi, as he convinced him that I was the person for the job. Fortune knew me and knew that I walked out of the Office of the Director of University Extension, after serving as administrative assistant for several years, without giving any notice. I did so immediately after President Nixon signed

Executive Order 11246 that stated federal regulations would be imposed on any institution accepting federal money. The chancellor called all administrators at the university to the Lyceum building for a meeting on how to implement such policies on the campus. I never knew what policies were discussed, but when the director of University Extension returned to his office, he announced that all women employed at University Extension would sign in each morning and sign out at the end of the day. All women but not the men! I simply picked up my purse and walked out the door. At the time I believed I had good reason for walking out without notice, but I later realized that I also closed the doors for further employment at the University of Mississippi. Chancellor Fortune knew this story, but somehow Tom Flynn convinced him that I was the one for the job with the new program. It was the beginning of twenty-four years with the Mississippi Humanities Council.

I was always ready to take another course, and after receiving my doctorate in 1975, I adopted the emerging philosophy that it should be stamped "For Five Years Only." In 1978 I applied to Harvard's Management Institute and spent five weeks on their campus. In 1985 I went with Peggy Prenshaw, professor of literature at Southern Mississippi University, to the University of London to enroll in her course on British Women Writers. While working with the public humanities program, I also attended two leadership seminars at Millsaps College. My quest for continuing my education began at an early age, and each course I pursued simply opened new doors for me. I do not intend for that quest to end.

I continued my involvement in women's issues while employed by the MHC. I joined the AAUW in 1961 and served as president of the Oxford branch, president of the

Mississippi AAUW, member of the National Board of AAUW, and vice president of AAUW Educational Foundation. I served as the first chairperson for the Mississippi Women's Political Caucus; program chair for Mississippi's observance of the International Women's Year; AAUW topic chairman for "Women: Agents of Change"; state panelist for the American Council on Education's National Identification Program for the Advancement of Women in Higher Education Administration; and chair of Southern Women in Partnership for Equity, a network of women in nine southeastern states. I worked very hard to secure credit for women, to get women on boards and commissions, and to get women involved in the political process. I even ran, unsuccessfully, for state auditor in 1991.

During 2008, I listened to the presidential candidates and the discussion of the questionable role of President Clinton in Hillary's campaign. I realized that even with the advancement of women in the past thirty years the married woman vying for a top position must show a role for her husband. The wives of the male presidential candidates needed only to play a supportive role.

In 1977, Mississippi University for Women searched for a new president. The school never had a female president, but a number of my friends wrote letters nominating me for the position. No doubt it was the letter from my major professor at Ole Miss, John Fawcett, which landed me an interview with board members of the Institutions of Higher learning.

Shortly after the interview began, they asked about my husband, a professor of biology at the University of Mississippi. Would he go to Mississippi University for Women? Well, I certainly had no job to offer him at that

time. Then came the big question, "Well, who will pour tea?"
We never got beyond the question of who would pour tea,
and the interview ended. I never had any problems claiming
bartenders; would it have been so difficult finding someone
to pour tea?

John R. Fawcett

My Supporters

Through the years, I claimed three of my council members to help me with the reception prior to each of the council's business sessions. I was careful to select members who were truly my friends, were committed to the business of the MHC, and were willing to prevent intoxication. Jack Gunn, dean at Delta State University, was my first bartender. He arrived at council meetings early and stayed until the last member left. His wife often accompanied him to the meetings.

I chose Aubrey Lucas, president of University of Southern Mississippi, as my next bartender. I was unable to attend the inflammatory conference leading up to the White House Conference on Families, but Aubrey moderated that meeting and received acknowledgement for his rare tact and firmness. I was sorry that I was not present to host a "drinking" panel afterwards. From the feedback I received, it would have been very appropriate. I was also most grateful to Aubrey for the "Tribute to Cora" which he drafted as I ended my presidency of the Mississippi Institute of Arts and Letters.

Father Saikley, head of the Greek Orthodox Church in Vicksburg, was a very close friend and our voice in Vicksburg, obtaining newspaper coverage for MHC events and activities. He was most gracious as he tended the bar and talked with council members. What he had to say on the council's behalf was quite telling:

21

It is a council of thinking people. Everyone on the
council cares about what we are doing. We are
interested in making our state the best it can be. And
let's face it, unless you are thinking, you can't be the
best.

He rarely missed a meeting, and Father Nick actively
participated in discussions and debates. The minutes reflected
more motions supported by Father Nick than by any other
member. He hosted a meeting in Vicksburg for the executive
director and civic leaders.

Paul McMullan, head of Unifirst Bank in Hattiesburg, was
not one of my bartenders, but as long as he was on the
council, he picked up the tab for the liquor served at our
receptions. When meeting at hotels, Paul said, "Sign my
name, Cora, but be sure to give a good tip to the waiters."
He also helped me establish a personal credit rating. While
on the council, I tried to borrow $2,000 in my own name
to redo my mother's kitchen. Three banks turned me down
because I had no credit rating. Paul heard about my dilemma
and stepped in with the Unifirst Bank in Jackson to get me
a loan. Then he suggested that Mary Libby Payne, dean of
the Mississippi College School of Law, and I do seminars at
his bank in Hattiesburg and at the bank in Jackson to inform
women about establishing credit in their own names. We
had credit cards with our names on them but found, due to
my experience, that the account numbers were the same as
our husbands'. We did the seminars, and Unifirst presented
Mary Libby and myself with crystal vases—men giving the
seminars would, no doubt, have earned cash. I found that the
vases were bought at McRaes Department Store, so I carried
mine back to get cash. Years later when we were on a panel

at the University of Mississippi, Mary Libby told this story, held up her vase, and explained that Cora opted for the cash.

Mary Libby Payne and Cora Norman

We NEVER spent public money on alcohol. Except for Paul McMullan's contributions, I paid for all alcohol and counted it on my income tax, costing me audits by the IRS for three consecutive years. Fortunately, I had meeting dates and receipts for expenditures which cleared me!

Lucy Somerville Howorth participated in only a few of our regrant programs but was a panel member on the program, "Exploring Options for Today's Women," sponsored by the Coahoma Humanities Committee. However, she was my mentor, and I called often to seek her advice. When I gave the honor's day address at Delta State University, she and her husband Mister Joe were in the audience. During my address, I mentioned the name of a person I admitted that I knew nothing about. The next day I received one of his books from Lucy to enlighten me! I spoke at her 100th birthday celebration in Cleveland and gave the following tribute:

We came today not only to celebrate with you a long journey, but more importantly, the type of journey you have charted. You planned and prepared at an early age for your journey, exemplifying that life should be actively creative with periods of peace to refresh the soul. Surely, you have been "the master of your fate and captain of your soul" by seizing those opportunities to make a difference in your world. Today we salute our fearless warrior who has championed so many worthwhile causes—especially for women. Lucy, little did you know when you spoke to a group of distinguished women at the White House in the 1940s and proclaimed yourself a FEMINIST, that in the 1990s your statement would give many southern ladies the courage to say, "We, too, are feminists!" For many of us, you have been our mentor, our leader, our role model. For all of us here, you have been a friend. Happy Birthday!

Lucy Howorth and Cora Norman
100th Birthday Party

When I campaigned for state auditor, I carried two counties—Lafayette, my home, and Bolivar, due to Lucy and her niece Keith Dockery McLean.

I am now retired and, of course, living on a budget, but I am rich indeed as long as I have friends like Lucy Howorth upon whom I can call. Some were never connected in any way to the state humanities program, but without my friends I probably could not have endured the years I did in my work.

Leslie McLemore, professor of political science at Jackson State University, and members of the Fannie Lou Hamer Institute at Jackson State University were often in my home for get-togethers. Leslie established the institute at JSU and made a name for himself throughout the state as he participated in more of the early MHC programs than any other professor.

Cora Norman (*standing*) with Fannie Lou Hamer Institute leaders. *Left to right:* Jeff Kolnick, Michelle Deardorff and Leslie McLemore.

John Peoples, a charter member of the MHC, continued to be my ardent supporter. When I brought my first computer home, he came to help me acquaint myself with the technology. Years later, when John asked if I had updated that computer, I had to answer, "No." He was disgusted with me for my lack of knowledge. However, when I received the Ageless Hero Award from Blue Cross/Blue Shield of Mississippi, John and Mary drove to Hattiesburg to be with me for that luncheon.

Left to right: John Peoples, Cora Norman, and Mary Peoples.

Senator Thad Cochran was a long-time supporter and was involved in women's programs. Through the years, he attended the federation's breakfasts in Washington, D. C., and prior to my retirement, we claimed one of the large Senate reception rooms for a federation meeting due to Senator Cochran's arrangements.

While living and working in Jackson, whether I was in need of a fun party or just consolation, there was a group of very close friends that always came when I called. I found that I called regularly. My list was not very long, but those on it, indeed, remain my friends today—Bobbye and Bill Henley, Mary Lou Payne, Bob Kochtitzky, Norma Fields,

Elizabeth Steen, Modena Martin, Bill and Lil Cooley, Doris Ginn, Marianne Hill, Tereza and Tom Holman, and Madel Stringer. Boyd Golding was also on my list, but sadly, he passed away in 2008. My friendship with Bobbye and Bill Henley began a very long time ago. During the 1970s and early 1980s, Bobbye and I constantly worked to improve the status of women. We had more get-togethers for politicians and community leaders than even we could remember. Before Bill and I left Mississippi in 2007, the Henleys hosted a going-away party which included many of our long-time friends. Since our move to Tennessee, Bill Henley calls often.

Bill and Bobbye Henley

Left to right: Cora Norman, Bill Minor, and Bobbye Henley.

Mary Lou Payne and Norma Fields both joined me on trips to the United Kingdom. Norma refused to drive after dark, but Mary Lou not only drove but made a new road for driving.

Back row, left to right: Modena Martin, Imogene Borganelli, Boyd Golding, and Cora Norman.
Front row, left to right: Norma Fields and Bobbye Henley.

Mary Lou Payne and Bobbye Henley

I also appreciated two who called regularly just to check up on me—George Williams and HelenSue Parish. Whether it was a good day or a bad day, HelenSue seemed always to get the news and call that night. She and her husband Bill Parrish, from Starkville, were great supporters of my writing this book. I am indebted to both. George Williams was my husband's graduate student at Ole Miss and remains a part of our family.

Cora Norman and George Williams

For years, working with the Margaret Walker Alexander National Research Board, I found that Robert Smith, M. D., was one of my greatest supporters. My first meeting with him was brief but unforgettable; while Mary Burciago and I planned a birthday celebration for Dr. Jessie Mosley, Robert hurried in and handed us a hundred dollar check for postage. I didn't know the man then, but through the years I came to rely on him very much.

During the last years in Mississippi, I discovered Will Long of Greenwood, who was much involved with the Mississippi

Institute of Arts and Letters. Because of him, Aubrey Lucas presented the wonderful "Tribute to Cora" at MIAL's 2007 Award Dinner, and I am deeply indebted to both.

From The National Foundation For The Arts And The Humanities To The Mississippi Humanities Council

With the advent of the atomic age in the 1940s, the sciences soared on our college campuses. By the early 1960s it was evident that with the support the sciences received from the national government, the humanities attracted fewer students. Certainly, the professors in the sciences had more opportunities than those professors in the humanities. Then, in 1965, Congress established the Foundation for the Arts and Humanities. The national legislation recognized that a democracy demands wisdom of its citizens, who need the abilities to reason, to think critically, to make judgments, and to deal with ambiguities in order to govern themselves. Although considered elitist by some, the study of humanities—linguistics; archaeology; ethics; and the history, theory, and criticism of the arts— provides the basic teachings of our culture and anchors us in our own society and civilization.

Congress appropriated money to the National Endowment for the Arts and to the National Endowment for the Humanities. The two became separate entities and directed their own programs. It was 1970 before the National Endowment for the Humanities recognized the need to initiate a program for the average citizen and pursued a state-based program. John Barcroft came to NEH from Brown University and stayed until all fifty states were sold on the idea, becoming the "father" of the state-based program. He pursued one state at a time and brought a group from each state to Washington, D. C., for a two-to-three day briefing on expectations for the state-based program. Reportedly, John talked and smoked incessantly.

Initially, they selected five states to do a pilot program and from their experiences took the initial steps to lay the basis for a state program. Barcroft stated that the state-based program had two objectives: (a) to have the humanities survive, and (b) to have society survive. The basic aim of the state-based program was to relate the humanities and the humanists to issues of concern of the people of the state through the following guidelines: (a) to concentrate on the humanities, (b) to deal with public policy issues, (c) to aim at the out-of-school population, (d) to involve academic humanists, (e) to relate programs to the state's adopted theme, and (f) to show matching funds.

The first year's grants to the state-based committees consisted of money for the administration of the program and money for local programs. The committees selected local programs through a proposal process and called the money provided a "regrant."

Mississippi was about the 15th or 16th state invited to participate and received approximately $50,000 for its planning stage. The accompanying mandates stated that meetings involving local citizens be held throughout the state to identify current issues, that the committee directing the program be enlarged, and that a theme from the identified issues be adopted to which future programs would relate.

In December 1971, Porter Fortune, chancellor of The University of Mississippi; Tom Flynn, professor of philosophy at UM; Parham Williams, dean of the Ole Miss Law School; John Bettersworth, vice president of Mississippi State University; and Estus Smith, dean of Liberal Arts at Jackson State University, who represented John Peoples, president of JSU, spent two or three days in Washington, D. C., with John Barcroft and officials at the National Endowment for the Humanities in orientation for the humanities program in Mississippi—four whites and one black.

The Mississippi Humanities Council formed early in 1972 with those five original members who went to Washington. They enlarged the group, selected a staff administrator, and held five public meetings throughout the state to identify pressing issues. The primary issue facing the state at that time was the education of its citizens; it continues to be the primary issue to this day.

After returning to Mississippi, Tom Flynn discussed the administrator position with Porter Fortune and informed me that I had the job. I knew that I had to sell myself to the other three—Parham Williams, John Bettersworth, and Estus Smith. Parham knew me and at one time even offered me a job at the law school, but that was before I walked off the job at University Extension. However, I knew that he accepted the chancellor's decision.

I drove to Starkville for an appointment with John Bettersworth at Mississippi State University. He received me in a most professional manner, but it was not a warm reception. However, John became a steadfast and committed member of the Mississippi Humanities Council and was most supportive of my work with the council. I left Starkville and drove directly to Jackson State University to meet Estus Smith.

My first visit with Estus was the beginning of a life-long friendship, and my admiration for him grew through the years. He could not have been nicer that day. He got up from behind his desk and came to the front to sit while we talked. I left feeling that it was, indeed, a successful visit.

When I left Estus Smith's office, it was mid-afternoon. It was my first visit to a predominately black college campus, but it was time for a cup of coffee, so I thought why not go to the student union and treat myself. I made my way into the student union and noticed that only young, black males were in the room. I immediately felt that I was getting the "once over." Admittedly, I never finished that cup of coffee. Years later, after many, many trips to black colleges, I realized that those young men were probably not paying me the slightest attention. Estus never stopped reminding me that my course in black history began that day.

I met with the original five Mississippians on the campus of The University of Mississippi in March 1972, and they composed a list of prospective council members for me to contact. The officials at the National Endowment for the Humanities suggested a council of no more than twelve persons. I knew only one name on that list— Sarah Rouse, professor at Mississippi College. I started calling, and not one person turned me down. However, before I could call Hodding Carter, editor of the Greenville newspaper, he died. Since every person on my list accepted the offer of membership, Mississippi started with the largest council of any state at that time—eighteen persons. Later councils followed Mississippi's example.

Not long after I took the job as staff administrator for the Mississippi Humanities Council, I went to Washington for my indoctrination at the National Endowment for the Humanities and to present myself to John Barcroft, the director of Public Programs at NEH. I was well aware of my lack of background in the humanities. I majored in chemistry for my undergraduate degree, physics and chemistry for my masters' degree, and would complete my doctorate in administration of higher education. I was ignorant of what the humanities included. After Tom Flynn first telephoned me about the position, I hung up the phone and went immediately to the dictionary to look up *humanities*.

Due to what I knew was my deficiency, I was uncomfortable about my appointment with John Barcroft. Thank goodness two staff members of Public Programs, Carole Huxley and Len Oliver, went with me to Barcroft's office. At that time NEH had specific stipulations when giving a state federal dollars for a humanities program: (a) programs were to target out-of-school adults, (b) public policy issues were to be addressed, (c) professors in the humanities were to be involved, (d) the federal dollars were to be matched with in-kind contributions if not cash, and (e) all programs were to be evaluated by the audience.

Unfortunately, but luckily for me as it turned out, on the morning of my appointment, the director of the Florida program called and took issue with the mandate that all programs would deal with public policy issues. Barcroft was quite aggrieved when I entered his office. He immediately said, "YOU will deal with public policy issues!" That order was repeated over and over again during the hour or less that I was in his office. Frankly, I was quite relieved. I was involved for several years in public policy issues in Mississippi through the American Association of University Women and the civil rights movement. I feared that I might be questioned about writers of literature and philosophy, and I knew I was not knowledgeable in that area.

Leaving Barcroft, Carole, Len, and I went straight to Carole's office. They were both aware that my meeting with the director of Public Programs was not typical, and both were most solicitous of my feelings. We immediately went to the closest pub for consolation. However, in the long run, my situation that day with John Barcroft paid dividends in my future dealings with members of the staff at NEH because I saw them as humane and compassionate; I saw them as friends.

We had from March until August 1972 to meet with civic leaders, educators, and members of the public throughout Mississippi to determine the most pressing issues facing our state. Five public meetings were scheduled. Council members in each area were much involved in setting the programs' agendas, issuing invitations, and hosting the meetings. At the University of Southern Mississippi, I had Linwood Orange, professor of English, and Charles Moorman, administrator. At The University of Mississippi, Porter Fortune, Parham Williams, and Tom Flynn took the reins. John Peoples and Estus Smith promoted a program at Jackson State University. Jack Gunn, dean at Delta State University, and Matthew Page, our black physician from Greenville, hosted a meeting at Delta State. John Bettersworth turned the job at Mississippi State University over to Peyton Williams, professor of literature, and John Peterson, professor of sociology. Both Peyton and John later became members of the council and were much involved in the program until their deaths.

With the greater black population in the Delta, we knew the initial program planned at Delta State University had to include both black and white citizens. Jack Gunn was to host the meeting. I called Matthew Page, and he agreed to meet Tom Flynn and me in Jack's office to make plans for our public meeting. Matthew came and promised his help with the black community.

On the way back to Oxford that night, I ran over a dog. Tom was a real dog lover. He asked that I stop and then took off into the field by the road looking for the injured animal. Finally, he returned to the car and told me the dog was dying. A former priest, he prayed for the dog and insisted that we find the owner. I stopped at a roadside store, but they knew nothing of a stray dog. I then drove up a lane where we saw some houses. Tom continued to pray until I stopped in front of one of the houses. He got out of the car to knock on the door and stepped into a ditch into water that came up above his ankles. He forgot his prayer and let the profanity roll. I was afraid the people in the house would come out and shoot both of us. But they didn't, and they knew nothing about the stray dog, so we continued on our way to Oxford. Even with his wet feet, Tom still prayed for the dog.

Tom Flynn was really the father of the Mississippi program. During our first years, while we were at The University of Mississippi, he never missed an opportunity to speak for the humanities program. He was always ready to go wherever there was a possibility of a program. Tom participated in many of the programs and was one of our first ethicist scholars-in-residence in the hospital in Tupelo.

At each of the five initial meetings we worked to have both black and white citizens, most unusual at that time in

Mississippi. However, at the meeting in Hattiesburg at the University of Southern Mississippi, we attracted only one black woman, Dr. Melerson Guy Dunham, who retired from Alcorn State University. Dr. Dunham listened to what we offered and began her involvement with the Mississippi Humanities Council. She always claimed an audience whether she held her programs at churches or on the campus of Prentiss Institute. Her scantly written proposals always received funding because she involved some of our best known professors in the humanities, dealt with burning public issues, and drew large crowds of community people to her programs. Once, she had a proposal funded to a Methodist church, and she called about a film she wanted to show. Always concerned that we keep a separation between church and state, I asked Dr. Dunham, "How will the Jewish people react?" She replied, "They are going to be home." Dr. Dunham became a very good friend.

After we held the initial five meetings in 1972 to solicit the burning issues the attendees believed faced Mississippians, we found educational issues topped the list. We adopted the theme "Education: New Horizons for Mississippians." Education remains a top issue in Mississippi and has since the mid-sixties. In July 2005 Sid Salter wrote in The Clarion-Ledger, "There are more than 30 counties in Mississippi in which 25-56 percent of the 25-44 year old age group hasn't completed high school."

In August 1972, after putting our first proposal into the mail to Washington, I rushed to the bookstore on the campus of the University of Mississippi, spent the few dollars remaining in our initial grant for necessary office materials, and took off for my first visit to Europe.

John Barcroft

Upon returning from Europe, I had a letter from John Barcroft at NEH dated August 15, 1972: . . . This is a rather personal letter. . . I wish, however, to have it shared with the Mississippi Committee . . .

> I read the Mississippi proposal yesterday, and I am rhapsodic about it. All in all, it is the most honest and persuasive proposal we have ever gotten in this program. . . But what I want you to know now is that this proposal—and the energy of the Committee, and its staff, and the good people who gave you their ideas which led to the proposal—is a really important contribution to this program nationally.

> . . . It offers an example of how a serious committee and its staff do the initial planning for a solid program. We can use this as we discuss the program with state groups where the program is just beginning. . . The Mississippi proposal delivers on the rhetoric we have used so earnestly in behalf of the humanities at this

agency over past years. We, too, wonder sometimes whether we can succeed in moving from rhetoric to reality, whether this program really can touch— and reaffirm—some hopeful aspects of American life. The Mississippi proposal (and the work which preceded it) make [sic] it easier for us to insist that it can—perhaps even that it already is. . .

Carol Huxley, program officer at NEH, was our liaison and ardent supporter as evidenced by the following letter written August 25, 1972:. . .

While you have been gone, the staff here has had a chance to read over the proposal, and the atmosphere is positively euphoric. You and the committee have done a superb job, (as I knew you would) and the committees in the planning stages are already benefiting from having copies of the proposal to read over. . .

The Mississippi Humanities Council was off to a good start.

Porter Fortune, Chair: 1972-1977

Porter Fortune

Our first annual grant began October 1972. Of the original five persons invited to Washington, D. C., by the National Endowment for the Humanities to meet with John Barcroft, three were from the University of Mississippi. Chancellor Porter Fortune graciously provided space for the new Mississippi Humanities Council and allowed staff the same benefits as his Ole Miss staff. I discovered later that Porter really stuck his neck out by allowing those benefits. After retiring and receiving a monthly check from the Public Employees' Retirement System of Mississippi, I again appreciated the five years at Ole Miss when we paid into the state retirement system. Everyone simply assumed that Porter Fortune would chair the council.

Although faced with many challenges from the outset, I was enthusiastic and committed. The accolades our proposal received in Washington certainly helped. I had two main objectives prior to obtaining proposed programs for funding: (a) to recruit professors in the humanities who would leave their campuses and participate in community programs addressing the involvement of their disciplines in current public policy issues and (b) to identify nonprofit groups who would submit proposals for public programs involving public policy issues and professors from the humanities. However, I soon found I had an even bigger challenge. Leaders of the non-profit groups throughout the state had no idea of how to write a proposal or of our expectations. Certainly, the professors were leery of leaving the lecture system and academic setting to meet with Mississippi's out-of-school adults in a community setting. We later found that other states had the same problems: the cool response of academic humanists to participating in community programs, the need for more professors, and the struggle for proposals. We had to prove our commitment to such a program and to the institutions of higher learning because they were silent about their professors participating in such a program.

I lived in Oxford throughout the 1960s and knew that Mississippians were not yet accepting integrated programs. Federal funds were "tainted" because acceptance of these monies mandated the programs be open for all citizens. Yet, with a population made up of approximately 35% blacks, I made the commitment to strive to ensure that the black community got 35% of the federal monies that were dispersed. I also felt that the Choctaws should be included. As I looked back, I realized that I set impossible goals for myself.

Let me point out what living in Mississippi in 1972 was like. Desegregation in our public schools was new. However, the result was not integration throughout the state, as many private schools sprang up. The Holmes County school system, with approximately 5,000 students, had less than twenty white students following desegregation. The situation was about the same in Tunica County.

Even though the council chose education for the state's theme in funding proposals, our educational administrators were uninterested. Our school superintendents had their hands full trying to keep their schools calm and had no interest in inviting parents to come to their schools in the evening for a public humanities program. I was always a social person, and the cool reception I received when I attended the annual meeting of the state school superintendents on the Gulf Coast in 1973 was memorable. I initiated the invitation in order to tell the superintendents about the new Mississippi program. My mother was with me, and after the session in which I spoke, not one superintendent came by to speak to me. Although Mother never associated with educators, she thought it was not the way to treat her daughter.

Regardless of who received funding for their programs, we mandated the programs be open to all persons. We found few places where blacks and whites could sit down together. Campuses were open to all people, but in local communities it was a different situation. The council funded a proposal submitted by David Jones, assistant superintendent of education for Holmes County, for a radio program in his county. A different program aired weekly and involved professors from almost every institution of higher learning in Mississippi. The council even provided funds for installation of a telephone at the radio station to allow listeners to call in while the featured professor was in the studio. No one called. When I called the radio station and asked if anyone was listening, the reply was, "Oh yes. We do get calls asking when the next program will be aired." After one year of radio programs, we funded David for more programs to be held in the Community Room on the square in Lexington, Mississippi. There was some progress.

Dr. Peggy Prenshaw, professor of English at the University of Southern Mississippi, was much involved from the early years of the state-based program. She participated in an early program in Holmes County. On the way, she stopped in Mendenhall, Mississippi, and picked up her father to go with her. Near the school, she stopped for gasoline for her car, and her father asked the attendant for directions to the high school. The attendant answered, but Peggy knew she was going to the predominately black school, not to the white high school. With that correction, the gas station attendant turned and apparently wanted no part in giving directions to the school for blacks.

Professors never participated in public programs bringing their disciplines to bear on public policy issues. Few ever received invitations into community programs except, perhaps, a few from the music departments of our institutions of higher learning. At the December 1972 meeting of the council, we garnered 20 proposals for evaluation. John Barcroft attended that meeting and spoke of the rationale behind the state-based humanities program:

> To explain the humanities is difficult. The first question asked: What are the humanities like and what use do they have to society? We must concentrate on public policy issues. There are pragmatic reasons

why we should deal with public policy issues: to reach a broader segment of the population and to make the role of the council a missionary one in that the council must be homogeneous in thinking this program deserves a fair test.

At that time in Mississippi, fewer than 50% of our population even finished high school, and most of our adult citizens had no idea of what the humanities were. With so many of our adult population uneducated, a humanities program had very little appeal to community persons. The basic aim of the state-based program was to relate the humanities and humanists to issues of concern identified by the people of the state.

We were indebted to librarians throughout the state for coming forth and proposing programs for their communities. Jim Anderson, librarian at Hernando, was one of our early promoters. Others were Beverly Herring at Canton, Lucille Rogers at Amory, and Jane Bryan, librarian at McComb at that time.

As I went into communities throughout Mississippi during those early years, I always mentioned our chair, Porter Fortune. I found that using Porter Fortune's name gave legitimacy to the program even in his absence. The fact that he was chair of the newly organized humanities council also made a big difference when I set about the task of calling persons to constitute the membership of the first council. However, if I found myself in a black community, I mentioned that John Peoples, president of Jackson State University, was very involved in the program.

In later years, we found that we had insufficient monies for funding all proposals received. That was certainly not the case in the beginning. The recipients of our regrant monies were well aware that programs had to be open to all people and that no one was to be excluded.

Dr. Melerson Guy Dunham was much involved in the program from her first meeting with us in 1972 at the University of Southern Mississippi. Dr. Dunham was the only black person who attended that program addressing current issues facing Mississippians. From that day, until the day she was stricken with a stroke, she was much involved in the activities of the MHC. In fact, she worked on a proposed program the day of her stroke and refused to be admitted to the hospital until someone safely tucked the proposal papers underneath her body.

From 1972 through 1978 I worked closely with Dr. Dunham in all activities directed toward improving the status of people in Mississippi through education. She took people wherever they were and exhorted them to improve their minds in order to live more productive lives. For years I thought she had a house full of children, only to learn that she had none. She reached out and selected young people to call her children; I was a white daughter. I got my marching orders weekly and tried to do what she directed me to do. Born without advantages, Dr. Dunham took what God gave her—human dignity—and tried to instill dignity into others. She had no patience with timidity. She involved herself in civic issues for a better community, was a strong advocate for education, and committed herself to the mission of her church.

Melerson Guy Dunham

Dr. Dunham's book *The Centennial History of Alcorn University* was the first book authored by a black that the University Press of Mississippi published. She was one of the first black persons to hold membership in the Mississippi Historical Society. History was her area of study, and she coveted membership in that organization. In 1979 she received the Black History Award from the Mississippi Historical Society. When the Mississippi Women's Cabinet of Public Affairs opened its membership to black women, she joined. Today's young black people should know about this woman who opened so many doors in Mississippi so that they might live and work in the mainstream of all public activities.

The United Methodist Church planned to honor Dr. Dunham at a meeting in Virginia for her outstanding work with college campus ministries. She called to tell me she was uncomfortable receiving such recognition so far from home, as the people there might think she was an unknown black woman back in Mississippi. In the 1970s, Mississippi's image throughout the nation was quite tarnished. Dr. Dunham then directed me to send a telegram of recognition from Mississippi; I did just as she directed.

After her death, we hosted a luncheon at the Smith Robertson Museum and Cultural Center in Jackson to memorialize her. I learned at that luncheon that my long-time friend Doris Ginn was also one of Dr. Dunham's children.

Community groups in the past certainly held public programs addressing various issues, yet such programs were always either pro or con. NEH mandated we look at all aspects of the issues and give alternative rather than single solutions. Therefore, participants in our programs heard the history of the issue and different points of view but left without a definitive answer.

We tackled the task of getting professors involved. When we reviewed proposals during that first year, we found that too many lacked roles for the academicians. We began to hold workshops for professors and in 1973 held four separate Academic Humanist Workshops in different parts of the state, claiming 260 participants from 23 institutions of higher learning. The MHC funded 33 proposals by the end of the first year.

Then we focused on a state-wide, weekend academic workshop held in Jackson. On Friday night, Lieutenant Governor William Winter spoke. It was his first participation in the program, but, in the years that followed, he was very supportive of our efforts. I met with Estus Smith at lunch that day to finalize all plans for the workshop. I announced that a professor from Delta State University would entertain the group with Civil War ballads after the Friday night workshops. "CIVIL WAR BALLADS!" he exclaimed, and I realized then that my world up unto that moment was not the same as Estus' world. He said, "Don't you know that all the blacks will walk out?"

What a predicament in which I found myself. I never met Allen Dennis, the professor I invited over the telephone to perform for us, until late that afternoon when the professors began to register. I found myself going down the line in front of the registration desk asking, "Are YOU Dr. Allen Dennis from Delta State?" I finally found him. I hurriedly told him of Estus' prediction and requested he forget the idea of singing for the group.

Allen insisted that his songs had no racial overtones. Unconvinced, I ran to find Aurelia Young, who was in the music department at Jackson State University, and told her of my situation. I learned early that in situations which involved race Aurelia had a level head. Aurelia said, "Cora, I'll stay for the affair and sit on the front row." She did and held my hand. Allen Dennis was right, and we had NO trouble, but my friend Estus was already at home, having left me to cope with the situation.

Following a suggestion from NEH, we invited a council member from the Missouri program to be our luncheon speaker on Saturday—Gerald Dunne, professor at the St. Louis University School of Law. He impressed us with his presentation, and even though we had workshops following his address, I rushed to tell him good-bye as he left the motel. Dunne said to me, "I'm not feeling well and think I should check with a doctor before boarding the plane to return to St. Louis." I immediately got him into my car and took him to the medical school hospital located across the street from the motel. Personnel took him to an examination room, and I stayed by his side. His legs gave out and forced him to lie down. Then it involved his arms. As Dunne coped with a stroke, he kept telling me how sorry he was to put me through that ordeal with him. What a man! He gave me exact instructions to tell his wife as to where to find his insurance policies, and I called her with the information. Dunne remained in Mississippi for several weeks before he returned to his home in Missouri, and I visited him several times while he was in the hospital. For years I stayed in contact with Dunne and, on one of my journeys, stopped in St. Louis and met him and his wife for dinner.

We found that those in the community needed help writing proposals but knew it was a teachable skill. We engaged college and university professors as consultants and held proposal-writing workshops. We were indebted to many professors for helping us in this respect, but several from Delta State University participated. As it turned out, DSU professors wrote practically all the proposals the council received from the Mississippi Delta during its first years of funding. Michael Harrington, philosophy professor at the University of Mississippi, met with several groups in North Mississippi, but the council cited Clyde Williams at Mississippi State University and George Abraham at Hinds Community College for meeting with more community groups than any other community consultants. During the summer of 1974, we had 23 professors involved as community consultants, resulting in 49 proposals to the council—the largest number of proposals reviewed at one time. Their requests exceeded the amount of funds available for regrants. The council funded some but returned others for specific revisions.

The MHC held a week-end workshop for twelve humanities professors at the University of Mississippi. Their mission was to write model proposals that I might circulate to groups interested in funding. Some who attended were Ben Bailey, Tougaloo College; Peyton Williams and Clyde Williams, Mississippi State; and Aurelia Young, Jackson State University. I wish I recalled the other names.

Later, I discovered Robert Walker, a native of Vicksburg working on a doctorate in history at the University of Mississippi. Robert came to my office in the Bondurant Building and typed proposals complete with program titles, names of professors who should participate, and public policy issues to be addressed. I then got on the telephone, called librarians and other civic leaders, and asked if they would be interested in sponsoring such public programs. Invariably, they answered that they were unable to compose a proposal or that they had no time to work on such a project. I then explained that I could send them a proposal ready for the signatures of the project director and the financial officer. Many accepted and submitted the proposals to the council; ALL received funding.

Robert Walker
and Cora Norman

After the council discussed the proposals during the first funding session, Matthew Page suggested that we take the completed programs receiving satisfactory evaluations to other parts of the state in order to reach more audiences. Unfortunately, we always pushed for new proposals and ignored Matthew's suggestion. In looking back, I realized we should have done that differently.

Left to right: Estus Smith, Peyton Williams, Porter Fortune, Cora Norman, Jack Gunn, and Tom Flynn.

In those early days, we traveled the state telling our story of available money for public programs in the humanities. I received a letter from Troy Holliday, superintendent of education in Tippah County (Ripley). The one sentence letter read, "Please send me information about your program." I didn't wait for the postal service but jumped into my car, drove to Ripley, and sat on the steps of the courthouse, which housed his office, until he returned from lunch. Troy was hesitant to submit a proposal from only himself, so he involved the superintendents of education from surrounding counties. Their proposal included programs in all their counties and was one of the first funded by the MHC.

Barcroft forewarned us that the funding process would determine if the council was totally committed to discussing public policy issues. We found, however, that early proposals always identified the issues; it was the humanities in which they were weak. I felt, though, that if the programs involved the right professors, they would ensure the humanities would be brought to bear on the issues. When I returned a proposal that the council refused to fund because of the lack of humanities content, I received the following comment from the project director. "You told us that the humanities could address public policy issues, so you show us and not ask us how this will be done." A very good point I thought.

Throughout the first years, we had workshops for academic humanists and workshops for proposal writers to ensure proposals met NEH guidelines. When we at last received acceptable proposals, the council made the first regrant to Meridian Junior College. Jack Shank, professor at Meridian Community College, was the project director, and Linwood Orange, a charter member of the MHC, was a participating scholar. Tom Flynn and John Peterson were instrumental in writing a proposal submitted by the Choctaws, who received an early regrant of $3400 in August 1973.

The charter members of the MHC were all involved in some way in promoting the programs. The humanities professors on the council participated in programs without remuneration. Our administrators Chancellor Porter Fortune, Hinds Community College President Robert Mayo, John Bettersworth, and John Peoples publicized the council in television and radio spots, while Mayo also introduced us to members of the business community.

Although David Sansing, professor of history at the University of Mississippi, was involved in the early days of the program, it was 1978 before he became a member of the council. My office at Ole Miss was in the Bondurant Building, as was David's. He was usually in his office every Sunday, and I remembered him sitting on the steps of the Bondurant Building one Sunday when I went in to work. We discussed the launching of the new Mississippi program. He said, "Cora, keep a journal of your activities." I did for about three weeks, and today I'm truly sorry that I failed to follow David's advice. However, my days were long, and I had no secretary. I simply gave up the journal.

David Sansing

Hinds Community College received funding for a program in which George Abraham, professor of literature, served as project director. They held the program at the Holiday Inn near Millsaps College in Jackson, and it was unforgettable. George installed TV monitors throughout the room so people could easily see and hear the speakers. Robert Mayo, president of Hinds, got up to welcome the people, but nothing came through the speakers. It was an example of technology breaking down but the humanities remaining as Robert continued with his prepared welcome. I must add that George quickly corrected the situation.

George Abraham was a participating scholar throughout our early days, but he left the state and became dean at Ferris

State University in Michigan and later a business consultant in New York City. In 2007, he wrote *The Seven Deadly Work Sins Against the Golden Rule*, a MUST for all to read—students, academicians, organizational personnel. George pointed out that in all relationships—in the home, in schools, and in the work world—it pays to practice the Golden Rule. This book is so pertinent to today's world. George wrote me that the idea for the book started with his involvement with the Mississippi Humanities Council—"the teachers of humanities must contribute to the world of work."

Even though project directors always worked toward larger audiences than usually materialized, the public registered positive responses to the programs. The problem often was getting an individual to take responsibility for coordinating the programs; citizens attended willingly. Too often, we found the project director had no desire to do a second proposal; the first proved more work than anticipated and there was no remuneration. Many of the program evaluations indicated that the participants thought the regrant program worthwhile and hoped there would be more programs. Two early programs funded by the MHC—to Central Mississippi, Inc. and to the American Association of University Women—held more meetings than originally planned because of the enthusiastic response from the public. I must inject that for twenty-four years I read every evaluation of our regrant programs.

The black community usually had better attended programs than those in the white community, and, in some places in Mississippi, the humanities programs were the first racially mixed community programs outside of the public schools. During the council's first year, I heard that Edward Bishop was a well known leader in the black community in Corinth.

I invited him and his wife Eva to a program held at the University of Mississippi and then to a reception at my home. They came—the only blacks in the group that night. From that night on, I forever called on Ed Bishop to help with some program initiative.

Ed had several regrant programs in Corinth. At one, a carload of citizens opposed to the TVA nuclear plant located near Corinth in Athens, Alabama, attended. They questioned the program panelists that night about the effects of the nuclear plant on their community. Seven professors were on the panel, but no one knew anything about the nuclear reactor. As there were no scientists in the group, no one could answer such questions. Finally, Ed got up and assured them that he was ". . . confident that Dr. Norman will fund another program with scientists who can answer your questions." I was so relieved to get out of Corinth that night!

In 1974 Peyton Williams assessed the programs as follows: "There has been not enough controversy in some programs, not enough humanistic content in others, too much of the expert lecture in some, and too much of the easy-going 'bull-session' in yet others." So, we continually worked with both scholars and project directors to improve.

Other than some library programs that dealt with current issues and Southern writers, it was the public policy issues that generated the most interest and attendance from the general public. At the Evaluation Conference held in November 1975, the project directors pointed out the need to focus on public policy issues when publicizing the programs. They also cautioned that titles used in promoting the programs should be of general interest rather than academic in nature in order to attract lay citizens. In those early days, I persuaded a League of Women Voters friend, Virginia Harrell from Vicksburg, to write a newspaper article for us. When I read her article, I found she had not used the word *humanities*. When confronted, she replied, "The readers would not know what I was talking about."

Perhaps unknowingly, I helped in the desegregation of our programs. If a proposal came from a white organization with only white professors involved, I suggested that they also involve a black professor. If the proposal came from a black organization, I suggested that it also include a white professor. The two professors frequently added to the programs were Leslie Burl McLemore from Jackson State University and Peggy Prenshaw from the University of Southern Mississippi.

We needed publicity, but as a staff of one, I was so busy meeting with civic leaders and professors around the state that I fell short on publicity. After meeting with a group, I dictated into my tape machine while driving back to the

Left to right: Dr. Tom Flynn, Rubye Lyells, George McLean, and Dr. Jefferson.

office, and the next day I acted as secretary and translated and typed the messages. However, in 1973 the council employed Jim Jeffries to produce ten TV spots that were carried by some of the TV stations in the state.

George McLean, editor of *Northeast Mississippi Daily Journal* in Tupelo, was involved in our initial programs soliciting input for issues facing the state. However, after our first year's funding, I called him to ask for his continued assistance. He replied, "Cora, your program is not worth a cup of hot spit." I knew he was quite an activist and had no patience talking about all aspects of an issue—just move on to the solution. When I hung up the telephone after my conversation with George, I knew I had to try again.

Just prior to this incident, Troy Holliday sent an evaluation from one of his Tippah County programs in which local Chancery Judge William H. Anderson commended the program:

> That was one of the most interesting and informative educational meetings that I have ever attended. The information and thoughts that were brought out by the various speakers were most interesting and stimulating. I have been very interested in education throughout my life, having served for a while as Acting County Superintendent of Education of Tippah County, as a member of the Board of Trustees of an Agricultural High School, for many years as a member of the Board of Trustees of a Junior College; and as an attorney representing various consolidated and municipal school districts, the County School Board, etc., and there were constructive thoughts

brought out at the meeting mentioned that I had never heard in any of these connections.

That group of sponsors had a clear understanding of what the educational process is all about, and what it should be about, and I only wish that all of the people of the county, particularly parents with children in school, could have the benefit of the speakers that appeared on that occasion.

I immediately called Troy and asked if he would meet me in McLean's office in Tupelo that afternoon. Troy agreed without hesitation, and we met later that same day with George. Whether we convinced him or not that we needed him was unclear, but he certainly never used his newspaper against us.

Troy Holliday remained active in the program through the years and became a member of the council in 1993. After my retirement, I attended a meeting of mental health commissioners in Tunica and found Troy there. He later invited me to have a drink with a group of other mental health commissioners from his area.

Another misunderstanding we faced was the distinction between the arts and the humanities. Everyone thought they knew what the arts encompassed but had no idea what the humanities meant.

The first Governor's Conference was in 1973 at the old Heidelberg Hotel in Jackson. The council rejected the initial proposal submitted by Dr. Milton Baxter, director of Education under Governor Bill Waller, but finally funded the conference. It took several revisions and the proviso that

Estus Smith monitor and approve all final arrangements. During that time, the State Department of Education also had a proposal turned down by the council, and Estus again met with the people in that department to revise their proposal.

Parham Williams, John Bettersworth, and Estus Smith comprised the council's first screening committee. They never invited me to attend their meetings. Parham always gave their findings and detailed recommendations to the council, and I sometimes wondered if Estus and John even read the proposals.

During the early years, we worked to get council members on television programs directed to local communities. I contacted the Gulf Coast television station, and Estus and I were given 15 minutes of their hour-long community program. With race relations volatile in Mississippi in 1973, especially outside Jackson, I feared what might happen to Estus if I rode to the Gulf Coast with him. I even feared he might be shot by a member of the Ku Klux Klan. Yet, it made no sense for us to drive two cars to the Gulf Coast, so I went to Porter Fortune with my dilemma. Porter said, "Cora, you go with him." We got to the television station, and Estus was so articulate that the director of that program gave us the entire hour. During a one-minute break, Estus turned to me and asked, "How do we get off this program?"

In early 1973, a newspaper reporter interviewed Estus about the humanities program and wrote, "Judging from the kind of council we have, the members who serve, and audience response, it is indeed a new day in Mississippi." The reporter cited the fact that Mississippi was a model for other state humanities programs and helped other states write their own guidelines. He added that several professors who participated in the program commented that they were surprised at the results and returned to their campus environments enriched by the experience. He quoted Estus, who said, "This is not the time to rest on our laurels, but to look to the future."

Estus encouraged people to involve the black colleges more fully. He said that when a black college held a council program, the white population seemed to feel uninvited. He found it hard to understand, especially at state-supported schools, and said that all tax payers should go out to see exactly where their money went. He also pointed out the need to include all ethnic groups, such as the Choctaws.

When NEH invited the original five Mississippians to Washington, D. C., Porter Fortune made an indelible impression upon John Barcroft. NEH held the first national meeting of the state humanities councils in Washington, May 1-3, 1973, and Fortune was one of three state chairs invited to address the group. NEH invited all council members to attend the Jefferson Lecture, recognition for distinguished intellectual and public achievement in the humanities, with travel expenses reimbursed. Several wives planned to attend. I began to make plans, as some of those attending never sat at a table with another race, and I wanted the entire Mississippi delegation to have dinner together those two nights in Washington.

For that first night, I reserved the Faculty Dining Room at George Washington University. I carried magnolia blossoms all the way from Mississippi to decorate the tables and invited all Mississippi congressmen and their wives to attend. Senator Stennis was recuperating from a gunshot wound, and the university roped off an entire block in preparation for his entourage. However, Stennis' legal advisor John

Hailman and his wife were the only ones to attend from the senator's office. Later, I received a letter from Hailman that stated how impressed Senator Stennis was with the council and how glad he was to support our efforts. Senator Cochran sent his regrets. David Bowen, representing the Second Congressional District, was the only congressman to attend.

There were about twenty persons from Mississippi attending the Jefferson Lecture the second night. Erik Erikson was the speaker, and we all had a hard time understanding him. Matthew Page, our medical doctor, finally advised us to shut our eyes so that our ears would pick up more. We did; it worked.

That night we had reservations at a seafood restaurant following the lecture. When we arrived at the appointed hour, our table was not ready. Several of us had drinks. Unfortunately, my husband, a teetotaler, accompanied me on the trip and insisted we go to another restaurant. Where do you take 20 persons for dinner at ten o'clock at night in Washington, D. C., without reservations? When they finally seated us, I turned to Matthew Page and said, "I'm sick!" Matt looked at me, smiled, and said, "You'll be all right soon." He knew my situation. Immediately, I jumped up and flew to the women's restroom. Sarah Rouse, another teetotaler, came to hold my head. After up-chucking, I returned to the table feeling fine once again. I shall never forget my friends Matthew Page and Sarah Rouse that night.

During the day in Washington, we met with NEH officials who planned the agenda and did all the talking. At the last meeting, our own R. A. McLemore rose and thanked NEH for the meeting and for picking up the travel expenses. It seemed that no one else thought of such an act.

The planned meals went well, and we were finally on our way to the airport to return to Mississippi when Tom Flynn announced he had no return ticket. I bought the tickets originally, so I knew he had one. Arriving at the airport, he checked his bag, assured that he would be seated even without a ticket. Tom was a priest for many years, and apparently others always handled such details for him. The ticket agent was not so cooperative and finally ordered his luggage removed from the plane. When Tom retrieved his bag and searched its contents, he found his lost ticket.

Tom Flynn and Cora Norman

I can't refrain from sharing another episode about Tom Flynn and his plunge into the life of an ordinary citizen. He came to the University of Mississippi from California, where he lived for years following his education in New York. He certainly knew nothing about life in Mississippi. During his first months at Ole Miss, he lived with Dean of Liberal Arts Arthur Lewis and his wife. Every weekend, Tom took off on his motorcycle to explore the state. One such exploration found him at the Neshoba County Fair. He entered by way of the carnival activities. Dressed in his usual white suit,

Tom walked by one of the booth attendants who hailed him to come and take his chances at identifying the shell that covered the nut. He immediately lost all his money, turned to the man behind the shell game, and asked where he might cash a check. Who went to the Neshoba County Fair in Mississippi in 1973 and asked a carnival attendant where to cash a check? Perhaps today we might use a debit card!

Tom was always involved in the early regrant programs, most complimentary toward myself and the council, and enthusiastic about the future of the program in Mississippi. In July 1973 I received a personal letter from Tom Flynn saying:

> I am sanguine enough to think that in another ten years friendly colloquies among academic humanists and people in the many towns of Mississippi will not be a rare occurrence. If this becomes true, it will be due, first of all, to the vision and enterprise of the officials at the NEH which first envisioned and stimulated this state-based program; secondly, to the members of the MCH, who have given time, effort and prudent guidance to the program; thirdly, to the diplomacy, skill, and organizational talent of the staff administrator who has kept an 18 member committee working harmoniously together; fourthly, to the Washington coordinators, Mrs. Carole Huxley and Dr. Nathan Sumner, who have regularly replenished us with a national viewpoint and the experience of other states; and lastly to the Grants Office at NEH, which has not denied legitimate requests from the Mississippi Committee.

One afternoon I found Tom Flynn rushing from his office to get to Natchez to participate on a program we funded on venereal disease. I asked what a philosopher was going to talk about on that subject, and he replied, "Love." Tom served as our first scholar-in-residence as an ethicist.

I worked very hard during our first year to secure proposals that the council would fund and to utilize the funds given by NEH. When we received notification of our second year's funding, I was almost in tears and immediately called Porter Fortune. At $275,000, it was one of the largest grants given by NEH; how could we use that sum! Porter was delighted and told me so. I knew I was the one who had to get the job done, and early in the game I was unaware of how much I could depend upon the council members.

In 1974, Rust College recognized the work of the council. At their Founder's Day program that year, Rust awarded citations to Porter Fortune, John Peoples, and myself for involvement with programs funded by the Mississippi Humanities Council.

Michael Harrington, professor of philosophy at Ole Miss, was one of the first professors involved in public humanities programs, although he became a member of the council just prior to my retirement. He spent a day in Tunica and at Parchman Penitentiary in the role of community consultant, and the following day I received a long letter detailing the day's events.

Michael arrived in Tunica, and the superintendent immediately took him on a sightseeing tour to the Mississippi River. Just before reaching the river, they got stuck. After a quick lunch at the home of his host, Michael had a chance to admire and play slot machines that his host renovated. In his letter, he asked, "Cora, under what category do I list my gambling losses on my expense report?" His new-found friend assured him that he would back the proposed program, which they never discussed, and would ensure an audience for two programs.

Michael was then off to Parchman, where he apparently spent much time wandering the grounds of the penitentiary looking for Chaplain Howell. He then had to establish his identify before discussing the program for both inmates and correctional officers. He concluded his letter with the following:

> An uneventful trip back to Oxford culminated in a mad dash to the tub, where I proceeded into the first of two day's worth of washing off the dirty asphalt and sand embedded in my hair, on my arms, and down my back and neck. Let everyone be aware that bringing the humanities to rural Mississippi requires bringing humanists to the bathtub.

Since we dealt with educational issues in the first years of the program, I heard that the schools had a very real problem in the communication between white teachers and black students and/or black teachers and white students. I heard that Roy Hudson, a professor at Mississippi Valley State University and a great communicator, dealt with this problem and had the ability to slip from corporate English to the black dialect in the same sentence. I drove to MVSU and found that he was off campus but would be back that evening. I sat in his apartment until he returned home that night and then told him what we needed. We soon funded a program, arranged by Michael Harrington, for Tunica public schools and involved Roy as the humanities professor.

With desegregation, Tunica county schools had about 5,000 students, and less than a dozen were white. Roy received so much admiration at that program that the school system invited him back more than once at their expense. He helped us with programs at Mississippi Valley and throughout the state.

Early in my work with the humanities council, I found myself much indebted to R. A. McLemore, a charter member of the council and a former president of Mississippi College. I knew R. A.'s wife Nannie through many years of working with AAUW but not R. A. However, I learned much from him. I never wrote him a letter without receiving a response, regardless of my message.

In the very first years of our existence, the blacks boycotted the businesses in Byhalia, Mississippi, and race relations there were very tense. I received a telephone call from a young man from Byhalia who worked in public relations at the University of Mississippi. He knew that we worked to establish communication between the races and requested we do a program in Byhalia. I took the request to the next council meeting, but the members told me to stay out of Byhalia, that we were not in the business to negotiate.

However, a federal agent finally went to Byhalia, and a biracial committee formed to bring stability back to the community. The president of that committee was a white minister who invited me to speak with them. I went. The committee later submitted a proposal signed by their president. A telephone call followed in which the president told me that if we

funded their proposal "all hell will break out in Byhalia."
Well, I had the proposal but no authority to deal with it. I
took it to the council and confessed my involvement. Dr.
McLemore immediately moved that "the proposal not be
funded due to limited funds." The motion passed without
any further comments, and no one said anything further to
me about Byhalia.

Porter Fortune welcoming
Executive Directors to First
National Meeting, Biloxi,
Mississippi, 1974.

In March 1974, the NEH
hosted its first national
meeting of state directors
and chose Biloxi,
Mississippi, as the site due
to Porter Fortune's influence
with John Barcroft. The
University of Mississippi
was the designated fiscal
agent. Porter and I urged
all Mississippi council
members to attend and
to host the cocktail party
planned for the opening of
the meeting. Porter Fortune,
John Bettersworth, Tom
Flynn, R. A. McLemore,
Linwood Orange, Matthew Page, and Estus Smith made the
trip to the Gulf Coast for the party. Estus acted as host for
Mississippi and stayed to attend the entire meeting of that
group. He even brought a group of musicians from Jackson
State University to entertain during the first evening's
reception.

Left to right: Estus Smith, R. A. McLemore, and
Cora Norman.

When I asked the staff at NEH what I might do to help with
the meeting, they replied, "Keep John Barcroft out of our
way." I kept a suite with a well-stocked bar open 24 hours a
day and made John the constant host. After the meeting, back
in my office in Oxford, I received flowers from Barcroft and
Carole Huxley. We also received many letters thanking the

Cora Norman welcoming colleagues to Biloxi,
Mississippi.

Mississippi council for being such hospitable hosts. I personally received a very complimentary letter from Lin Oliver, assistant director of State-Based Programs, Division of Public Programs, NEH. Lin gave me much credit for the success of the meeting—"You showed us how to make a conference of this sort work through personal efforts which went far beyond what normally could be expected." He further stated he thought it might also serve as a benchmark for all future meetings because of what I did to make it an enjoyable experience for everyone.

Porter Fortune also wrote a letter of thanks to Bruce Bellande in University Extension, which served as fiscal agent for the conference. In his letter to Bruce, Porter quoted what John Barcroft wrote to Senator Eastland:

> "We asked the Mississippi Committee for the Humanities to serve as sponsor of the National Meeting for two reasons. First, they have, in our judgment, one of the most effective programs in the country (and as you know, have been enthusiastically granted by the National Council on the Humanities the largest grant ever made in the state-based program). Second, as this will be an annual occurrence, we wanted the first meeting to be both business-like and stylish. You will be glad to know that it was.

Porter further stated in his letter that ". . . credit for the success of the meeting was due to Mrs. Norman, of our Mississippi Committee, and to the staff of University Extension. . ."

Later, at a national meeting in Washington, D. C., John Barcroft covered the Biloxi program well. He emphasized the councils' responsibilities of evaluating the humanities content of their programs, involving new members for new ideas, looking for other funding sources, considering sabbaticals for their staff, and by all means, keeping the congressional delegation informed. While in Washington, Estus Smith represented the Mississippi chair at a dinner at the State Department and frequently answered the question, "How is Mississippi doing it?"

Although the council sponsored academic humanists' workshops in 1973, it was the following year when we held our first workshops for project directors—one in each congressional district. Such workshops continued for several years. In 1975, an academic humanists' workshop claimed some of our most involved scholars up to that time. The group leaders were George Abraham, Hinds Community College; Price Caldwell and John Peterson, Mississippi State University; Michael Harrington, the University of Mississippi; Lizette Hurst, Coahoma Community College; Leslie McLemore, Jackson State University; Peggy Prenshaw, University of Southern Mississippi; and William Sullivan, Delta State University. The conference coordinator was Peyton Williams. In 1975, the council acted upon a suggestion from Dr. Sarah Rouse and requested I expand trips to each campus to meet with groups of professors in order to promote greater participation. At a project directors' workshop in 1976, Michael Harrington made the following statement:

> By their own admissions, humanists learn from the programs; audience response provides a different viewpoint from the "captive student" audience; scholars become acquainted with new geographic locales; and ideas of citizens outside the college community receive primary attention and may result

in an increased awareness of community feeling on
the part of the scholars.

In those early years, we often invited small groups of
citizens to meet with council members and the executive
director to get their reactions to the proposed theme for
future funding as well as to our funded programs. One of the
first such meetings held in 1974 claimed Judge Darwin M.
Maples, Lucedale; George McLean, editor of the *Northeast
Mississippi Daily Journal*; Senator Bob Perry; Dr. Melerson
Dunham, retired professor from Alcorn University; Andy
Carr, Clarksdale; Dr. Milton Baxter, Governor Waller's staff
for Education; Father Fogarty, Catholic priest in Carthage;
and Dr. David Jones, assistant superintendent in Holmes
County.

The council funded Dr. Baxter for several governor's
conferences regarding education. With the proposal for
a second Governor's Conference, Dr. Page questioned if
the council was setting a precedent and allowing itself to
become a political pawn. However, Milton was always
very cooperative when the council suggested changes to his
original plans, usually to add more humanities professors to
the program.

With all my personal efforts to get to as many parts of the
state as time allowed, we still needed additional staff. We
had only temporary workers, Ole Miss students who worked
part time. They included Robin Street, Ann Coleman, and
Robert Walker to name a few. They were most helpful, but
we needed another full-time staff member.

In 1974, Betty Duvall King resigned from the council
and became our second full-time staff person, an assistant

director. However, NEH rejected this action since neither of us had a background in the humanities. We had to find an assistant director who did.

About that same time, we asked the Office of Personnel at the University of Mississippi for a full-time secretary. They told us, "You don't even have a file cabinet; why do you need a secretary?" None of the offices at the university employed a black person at that time, but Sadie Clark, a graduate of Alcorn State University, had written to the Office of Personnel requesting a secretarial job after the University of Mississippi School of Law admitted her husband. When they got her application, they literally walked to my office to give me her name. I immediately called an AAUW friend, Vivian Tellis at Alcorn State University, who gave a glowing recommendation of Sadie. So, she joined us as our first full-time secretary in the summer of 1974.

Sadie took care of all the usual secretarial duties. However, she did much more; she made new friends for the program via personal and telephone contacts. The program attained statewide recognition due, in no small measure, to Sadie's personal involvement and attitude. She was the first black staff person at the University of Mississippi. She quickly mastered the internal bureaucratic system and made friends with all supervisory personnel. The council changed her job title to administrative assistant during her tenure.

Chancellor Fortune soon recognized what a public relations asset Sadie would be in his office. I told him, "Keep your cotton-picking hands off Sadie." Looking back, I realized what an injustice I did to her. Porter never pursued an offer but recognized what an asset she was to the Mississippi Humanities Council's work. Although Sadie left the MHC in 1977, I feel so fortunate that we remain in contact with each other via correspondence and telephone.

In 1975, we received Comprehensive Employment and Training Act (CETA) funds and hired three staff persons: Bill Lukas in my office at UM, Emilie White at MSU, and Patricia Newman at USM. These three were extremely helpful in planning and assisting with workshops and conferences and providing publicity for the council in newspapers and television spots.

My work with the Choctaws began early in the program when I first met with Chief Phillip Martin. Leaving the reservation after that first visit, I felt that he would refuse to work with a woman, so I immediately sent Tom Flynn to Philadelphia. He and John Peterson, already involved with the Choctaws, received funding in 1973. After getting to know Chief Martin, I realized that I misjudged him early on. I found that he, indeed, worked well with women; he just knew nothing about the humanities!

I served on the first Choctaw Heritage Council, whose funded program involved bringing a Native American scholar, Dr. Bea Medicine, from Dartmouth to speak. They planned a supper prior to her speaking. I knew that I wanted to observe that program but must admit that I knew nothing about our Native Americans except what I saw in John Wayne movies! I hesitated to go in time for supper, afraid that they cooked food in a "common pot." Should I wait until later and arrive just in time for the program? If I waited, darkness might cause me to get lost on the reservation. I decided to go early and simply not eat. Just as I parked outside Chief Martin's office, another car pulled up beside me. It was Estus Smith and one of his friends from Jackson. Was I glad to see them!

Well, we went to supper and found that the menu consisted of ham sandwiches, potato chips, and Dixie cups full of ice cream for dessert—just like any other southern community supper. I learned a lot about the Choctaws that night but much more about myself. I needed to learn to deal with different cultures! Phillip Martin made financial contributions to the council and, at that time, was the only Native American chief to do so.

In the early days, I learned that NEH officials kept the United States senators advised as to programs in their respective states. In 1974, Tom Flynn and I visited Senator Eastland and met Frank Barber, a member of Eastland's staff who informed me of that process. Frank became a real friend and forwarded to me copies of information the senator received from NEH. I later learned how important it was to keep our congressional delegation advised of our programs and of our needs and how much it benefited us. Because of Barber's attention to this issue and his knowledge of the Mississippi program, I always invited him to dinner when I was in Washington with my activities with AAUW. It was Frank who took me to my first and only lunch in the Senate Dining Room.

It was the late 1970s before the council faced the accusation of humanists being anti-Christian, but they discussed the use of the term humanist in a 1974 meeting. At that time, philosopher Tom Flynn objected to its use because of its implication of being militantly atheistic from *The American Humanist Manifesto*. Dr. Nathan Sumner, who attended from NEH, stated, "We are saddled with it—yet you may call them by other terms." John Peoples replied that the term academic humanist had enough tradition behind it that we shouldn't worry about the definition as given in the *Manifesto* and added, "We should not be swayed by temporary trends. Dogmas are often transitory." John Bettersworth pointed out that *The American Humanist Manifesto* was not that widely read in Mississippi.

However, as anti-government sentiments grew and we celebrated the Year of the Child, opponents attacked us as being sponsored by a government that intended to take our children out of their families. The following year, the Year of the Family, we funded local programs and then held a state-wide program at Hinds Community College to elect delegates to the national White House Conference on Families. I was not present, but the anti-conference factions, bused in from surrounding counties, obstructed that particular program. I heard it was a fiasco. In December 1980, the council passed a resolution that cited Aubrey Lucas, President of USM, for moderating the state conference with "rare tact and firmness." I later received a letter from Bob Wolverton, professor at MSU and a participating humanist in that program who stated it was the worst situation in which he was ever involved. The White House Conference never took place because a number of states were unable to define family!

Prior to the program described above, we had a regrant program on the Year of the Family in Carthage, Mississippi, directed by Father Fogarty. Four or five attendees came from McComb and objected to the meeting. We formed small groups for discussion, and after I introduced myself, one of the men from McComb said that the MHC programs dealing with women, the child, and now the family gave him nightmares. Obviously, *The American Humanist Manifesto* made its way to Mississippi!

Members of the council early recognized the need of getting business leaders involved in the program and sanctioned a Business Leaders' Conference at the Mississippi Power and Light Lodge in Jackson in early 1975. Ms. Sylvia Westerman, a CBS executive in New York City, gave the opening address. She did an excellent job of explaining what the humanities contribute to daily living. When the council evaluated that program, Porter Fortune asked what could be done differently in the future. George Godwin, a recognized business leader in Jackson, acknowledged women and minorities were well represented but suggested the conference expand regionally with less structure and much more time for the business leaders to talk. He pointed out that the academicians and the business people communicated less than originally hoped. Matthew Page commented that only time would tell the value of the meeting and that in time the business leaders would become more cooperative. Following that first conference, we made every effort to include our business leaders.

George Godwin and Cora Norman

Mississippi Power and Light provided a bartender for that business conference. I provided a case of liquor and admonished the young man to make the drinks weak—we wanted discussions, not drunkards. At the conclusion of the meeting, I picked up my liquor and found that he used so little that it amounted to only half a bottle. He listened and cooperated!

John Bettersworth worked with ETV to offer a series of "PRO-CON" programs addressing issues that faced the state at that time. Cliff Hodge, dean of the Ole Miss School of Law, and Shelton Hand, professor at Mississippi College School of Law, developed the programs. Aurelia Young, professor at Jackson State, quietly but effectively pointed out during the planning stage the need for strengthening the humanities content, resulting in a highly successful "PRO-CON" television series. It involved two scholars in each of the 60-minute programs shown twice each month for nine months; one scholar took the pro side and the other took the con side of the issue discussed. At the end of nine months, Bettersworth reported that the programs were highly successful; ETV received more calls than their phones could handle. John wanted a letter of appreciation sent to Shelton Hand and Cliff Hodge for the many hours they contributed without remuneration. The council provided a mere $100 payment to each.

In 1974, Dr. Matthew Page asked the council the following question:

> To which people are we directing this program? We are in a transition period in our state and our history, and this council has the means to cause an impact. The American dream is white, Anglo-Saxon, and does not include all people.

Matthew Page

It was interesting that such questions regularly came up in our council meetings. It seemed that such reflection helped the council to keep itself directed in the right way.

The first regional program for citizens of the South was in Nashville, Tennessee, in May 1976. However, Oliver Emmerich, editor of the McComb paper, birthed the idea in Mississippi during the September 1974 MHC council meeting. The minutes of that meeting showed that Emmerich introduced us to the work of the Southern Growth Policies Board. The board, composed of governor-appointed representatives from each of the 15 participating states, appointed a Commission on the Future of the South and mandated a report on the future of the South. Emmerich recommended a regional conference with follow-up discussion in each state. George Godwin indicated that the discussions would define the common needs of all states. Owen Cooper, politician and business leader, moved to commend the idea to staff to study legibility, cost, and funding sources. Shortly thereafter, I brought up the issue at a meeting of the southern executive directors in New Orleans.

The southern executive directors joined in favor of such a meeting. No doubt correspondence and telephone calls between the executive directors resulted in the southern directors having it on their agenda at the National Meeting of Executive Directors in Aspen, Colorado, in June 1975. The head of the Southern Growth Policies Board, housed in North Carolina, joined the southern directors to discuss the possibility of such a conference. He gave no appearance of enthusiasm. After much discussion, we decided that the report could not be the basis of a humanities program. We left Aspen thinking the idea was lost.

I easily recalled the Aspen meeting because of a most embarrassing moment. I always traveled with a liquor bag and kept it with me on airplanes. However, we flew from Denver to Aspen in a small plane that required placing my liquor bag with the other baggage. When we deplaned in Aspen, the attendant unloading the luggage grabbed my liquor bag and threw it down. I knew that was the end of some of my bottles. There was a Land Rover awaiting us, and I hastened to put my bags in the rear and get myself seated inside—the very first passenger. When the vehicle was loaded, the driver went to close the rear door and then announced that someone's bag was leaking, demanding that the owner claim the bag. I had to get out on the sidewalk in front of my national colleagues, claim that bag, and remove the broken bottle. Needless to say, I was embarrassed. However, that night I roomed with Daisy Brownstein from North Carolina, and prior to our going to sleep, there was a knock on our door. Daisy opened the door, and there stood Jim Noel, executive director of the North Carolina program. His chums sent him to buy the contents of my liquor bag! It was my contribution to THEIR evening.

Heading home from Aspen, several of us gathered together at the airport in Atlanta; the nearest bar was always our meeting place. A discussion for a regional program immediately ensued. In the short time that we were in the Atlanta airport, Jane Crater, executive director of the Tennessee program, invited us to have a meeting in Nashville in mid-August to continue discussing the challenges the South faced and the possibility of a regional conference.

For that meeting in Nashville, Jane invited the executive director and one council member from each of the southern states. Oliver Emmerich and I attended from Mississippi.

Jane planned dinner aboard a riverboat the eve of our meeting, and it was another memorable experience. I knew I was probably the oldest woman of all the executive directors, and that night I proved I was. I arrived in Nashville that afternoon and decided to shop for a dinner dress. It was my first dinner on a riverboat, and I wanted to be dressed for the occasion. I bought a beautiful, pink organdy, formal dress. All the other women were in blue jeans! Oliver Emmerich realized that I was quite embarrassed by my attire and stayed by my side all evening. More than once he told me how nice I looked. Or, maybe Oliver's thoughts were of women of his earlier days!

The business session the following day introduced many ideas for a regional program. However, no consensus seemed possible. We elected a planning committee to go into their own session and return with a definite plan. The members of the planning committee were William C. Havard from Virginia; Jane Crater from Tennessee; James Noel from North Carolina; Robert C. Whittemore, dean of the University College at Tulane University; and myself. When we assembled, we found we had an uninvited guest, a futurist from the West—what audacity to join us uninvited! After several hours, we reported back to the main body that we would definitely proceed with plans for a regional conference and that we would keep all states advised as to our progress.

We left Nashville with a date on our calendars to meet in Atlanta for our next planning session. In Atlanta, the futurist was again with us. We decided that he was not representative of the southern states, and we simply dismissed him. That was not a comfortable situation.

The committee had several meetings at the Atlanta airport. Plans for the regional program moved steadily with Jane Crater and Bill Havard taking the lead. Jane and I were the only female executive directors in the South at that time, and I felt very close to her. We made a trip to Washington, D. C., to solicit funds from NEH but received no funds and no encouragement. It was interesting to recall that the finalized program plans impressed NEH, and they then came forth with federal dollars.

John Barcroft was at the podium during the opening session of the regional program with several NEH staff members in attendance, including Mississippi's Clyde Williams, who spent that year in Washington. Put together by Bill Havard and Jane Crater, it proved the most worthwhile state-based program to that date, and, in my opinion, the best ever presented by the state-based committees—"Peoples of the South: Heritages and Futures."

Each participating state selected 16 citizens who were representative of elected officials, corporate executives, education, minorities, scholars in the humanities, statewide and regional organizations, and state-based humanities councils. Alabama, Arkansas, Florida, Georgia, Louisiana, Mississippi, North Carolina, South Carolina, and Virginia participated in the conference. Mississippi had one of the best delegations in meeting the criteria as outlined. Afterwards, I received a letter from Charles Deaton, a Mississippi legislator from Greenwood, who stated, "The Mississippi delegation was the most outstanding state group from the point of view of state leadership, interest, and qualifications for the topics pursued." Our group included the following:

Elected officials:
Charles Deaton of Greenwood, Mississippi House of Representatives
Aaron Henry of Clarksdale, Mississippi House of Representatives, head of NAACP in Mississippi;
Ed Perry of Oxford, Mississippi House of Representatives
Frank Smith of Jackson, formerly U. S. House of Representatives

Corporate executives:
George Godwin, Jackson
J.C. Redd, Jackson

Scholars in the humanities:
Estus Smith, JSU
Peggy Prenshaw, USM
Alferdteen Harrison, JSU

Education:
Katharine Rea, Gulfport
Milton Baxter, Jackson

Statewide and regional organizations:
Emmett Burns, leader in NAACP
Doris Barwick, Jackson League of Women Voters

Media:
Raymond McGrath, Jackson

State Council:
Tom Flynn, UM
Cora Norman, Jackson

The Mississippi delegation also included four blacks.

We wanted a working conference. All delegates participated in one of seven panels and stayed with that group throughout the conference. The panels addressed land use, education, work, politics, urbanization, health, and justice. Since it was a working conference, the following, leading scholars prepared focus papers in advance:

Politics:

George B. Tindall, professor of history, University of North Carolina

Education:

John Tyler Caldwell, retired chancellor, North Carolina State University in Raleigh and graduate of Mississippi State University

Work:

J. Earl Williams, director, Center for Human Resources, University of Houston

Land Use:

Frank Ellis Smith, Mississippi congressman 1951-62

Urbanization:

Blaine A. Brownell, chairman, Department of Urban Studies and director, Urban Affairs, University of Alabama at Birmingham

Health:

Dr. C. L. Hooper, vice president for Health Affairs and director, John A. Andrews Clinics, Tuskegee Institute

Justice:

Frances Grant Loring, Memphis, Tennessee

The panels met for two days, and reports from each panel were prepared for publication.

Politics:

Dr. Lewis P. Simpson, Louisiana State University

Education:

Dr. Estus Smith, Jackson State University

Work:

Dr. Alferdteen Harrison, Jackson State University

Land Use:

Anne Bartley, Arkansas

Urbanization:

Anthony J. Gagliano, New Orleans, Louisiana

Health:

Dr. Ronald A. Carson, University of Florida, Gainesville

Justice:

Hillary Rodham Clinton, Arkansas

All participants received a published report of the conference co-edited by William Havard and Jane Crater, and audio tapes of all the keynote addresses and Congressman Brooks Hays' dinner address were available. Throughout the conference, John Egerton, a free-lance writer living in Nashville, conducted interviews with noted participants.

WDCN-TV of Nashville produced a special television series entitled "The South with John Seigenthaler; Its People—Heritage and Future." Seigenthaler, in group discussions with noted southerners and experts on the issue in question, attempted to deal with some of the more pressing problems that faced the South, as well as the rest of the nation at that time. The Mississippians who participated on some of those tapes were Frank E. Smith, former congressman and TVA director, on "Land Use in the South"; Estus Smith, vice president of Jackson State University, on "Education in the South"; Ray McGrath, WJTV in Jackson, on "Mass Media in the South"; and Aaron Henry, co-chairperson, Mississippi Democratic Party, on "Justice in the South." A video tape also included John Barcroft, director, Division of Public Programs, National Endowment for the Humanities, on "Public Policy in the South." Barcroft ensured that all the state councils dealt with public policy issues. His argument was that the programs would claim grass root participants, and he was certainly right. If we had not dealt with public policy issues, we would never have gotten the programs off our campuses of higher education! WDCN produced and sold cassettes of those interviews around the South after the broadcasts.

I asked Jane Crater Hiatt to help me recall the significance of that conference, and she gladly did. In evaluations, the participants reported they learned much about the issue each had explored, much more than they had anticipated. Jane also recalled she had at most three hours of sleep each night during the conference and had several sleepless nights as she

Jane Hiatt and Cora Norman

worked on preparations for it. We claimed that the success was directly related to Jane's unswerving devotion to seeing the job done well.

At the July 1976 meeting of the Mississippi Humanities Council, George Godwin gave a summation of the regional conference. He had an extremely favorable impression of the conference and noted the excellent preparation and pre-conference planning, wide variety of expressed viewpoints, absence of extremists in any area, representation of all segments of society, and open and friendly atmosphere throughout the conference. George thought a follow-up program in Mississippi would be an excellent idea, and later we funded a conference in Jackson. Tom Flynn agreed with Godwin's assessment.

It was also noteworthy that Peggy Prenshaw participated in the panel on land use. Peggy was a professor of literature at the University of Southern Mississippi and later dean of the Honors College. She said she went to Nashville wondering what she might contribute to a discussion on land use but found that southern authors had much to say about the subject. After that conference, Peggy became our voice on humanities programs dealing with land use.

We all learned much at that memorable conference, and although I have been out of the humanities program for several years, I have not heard of another regional conference attracting the leadership of the Nashville conference. We were all indebted to Bill Havard and Jane Crater Hiatt for their hard work. The keynote speakers were, and remained, society's leaders: Dr. Samuel DuBois Cook, retired president of Dillard University in New Orleans; Wilma Dykeman Stokely, Tennessee writer; Brook Hays, politician from Arkansas; and David Mathews, now president of the Kettering Foundation. Many of the participants remain in the public domain.

We funded the program "The People of Mississippi: Their Land and Their Politics" to the Mississippi League of Women Voters. Those who attended the regional meeting in Nashville inspired it, and program planners included George Godwin, Ed Perry, Ann Abadie, Doris Barwick, Emmett Burns, Charles Deaton, Alferdteen Harrison, Aaron Henry, Ray McGrath, Peggy Prenshaw, Katharine Rea, J. C. Redd, Estus Smith, Frank Smith, and Fran Leber. An evaluator assessed the program as follows:

> The conference was a huge undertaking and a tremendous success! I contribute the success to the following: the inspiration of individuals who had attended the "Peoples of the South: Heritages and Futures" in 1976 who initiated the idea to the League of Women Voters State Board, and last but not least the participants and the speakers.

George Godwin was not only a valuable member of the council but a personal friend. I visited him and Donna often in their home in Jackson. George held court around their dining room table, and it was a stimulating place with drinks and never ceasing conversation. Their teenage children often brought their friends home and joined the conversation. When one group left, another might later appear. It also became a favorite place for Tom Flynn whenever he was in Jackson.

When the council recognized the need for a business person, they elected George. He helped with our first Business

Leaders' Conference and led us through our first management study funded by NEH. I was most indebted to George for showing me how to handle my business expenses on my income tax return. Since I generally bought the liquor for the receptions held prior to the council meetings, George taught me to buy a generous supply and take any excess home for personal consumption. He also recognized that we had not adequately involved the media and that it was absolutely necessary to the success of a statewide program.

At the 25th anniversary of the Federation of State Humanities Councils, Richard Lewis gave the history of the federation and claimed that the idea for such an organization grew out of concerns expressed by the Western councils. I must add another dimension to the history, because in Mississippi we first heard about the need for a national group through Porter Fortune. The rationale was that we needed a lobbying voice in Washington, D. C. Geoffrey Marshall at NEH later echoed this idea.

In 1976, we had a meeting of state-based chairmen in Seattle, Washington, and discussed the formation of a national organization of state humanities councils. Fortune was unable to attend, but John Bettersworth represented him. At that time, an ad hoc committee formed to delineate the purposes of the state-based program. When asked regarding the necessity of such a lobbying group, the members of the Mississippi council supported Owen Cooper in his reply, "If there is to be a national organization, I think we should be part of it and not outside of such a group." That summed up the feeling in Mississippi.

Then at a council meeting in March 1977, Fortune reported on the proposed organization and announced an April meeting in Birmingham to be hosted by David Mathews, then chair of the Alabama council. Ila Wells, professor of literature at Mississippi Valley State University, and Bill Pennington, professor at Delta State University, attended that meeting. Reporting back to our council, they recommended that MHC join the proposed organization on a trial basis, provided that funds for membership not come from our administrative budget.

Ila Wells also served on the screening committee with Kent Wyatt, president of Delta State University, and Newton James, businessman from McComb. After a freakish accident on the campus of William Carey College led to her hospitalization for a number of weeks, Kent and Newt called her daily to check on her status. While on the council, she participated in promotional conferences, scholars' workshops, regrant programs, and evaluation conferences. Upon retiring, she joined the faculty at Rust College. Ila was an early supporter of the Federation of State Humanities Councils and one of the most charming and admired ladies of the MHC.

Linwood Orange, charter council member and professor at the University of Southern Mississippi, was on many of our regrant programs and stressed at a council meeting that all members needed to attend regrant programs to evaluate humanists' contributions, relevance to issues, ability to stimulate thinking, over-all presentation, and uniqueness of contributions. Linwood also recognized the need for publicity for the council and directed a videotape himself for distribution to commercial TV stations.

The council granted me a three-month sabbatical to attend Harvard's Educational Management Institute. What a learning experience that was for a southern woman! My suitemates were Sister Mary Aquinas Nimitz, dean of Dominican College of San Rafael and daughter of Admiral Nimitz, who headed our naval forces in the South Pacific during World War II; Nancy Broderick, associate dean of the faculty of Educational Studies at Buffalo State University of New York; and Roberta Brown, vice president for planning at Arkansas College in Batesville, Arkansas. Stress caused me severe dental pain, so I went to a local dentist who said, "I've never looked into a mouth from Mississippi!" At Harvard, I felt outclassed, but my fellow participants [there were 107 of us] voted me social secretary of the class of 1978. The following year I hosted the class reunion with Paul Barrett at Massachusetts Institute of Technology in Cambridge, Massachusetts. For years, I kept up with my new-found friend Solomon Owolabi from Nigeria, and Bill Bondeson, there from the University of Missouri, later came to Mississippi to speak to the MHC.

While still housed at the University of Mississippi, I received a telephone call from Walter Washington, president of Alcorn State University in Lorman, Mississippi. He asked why Alcorn State had no representative on the council and cited members from Jackson State University, the University of Mississippi, Mississippi State University, Delta State University, University of Southern Mississippi, Mississippi College, and Hinds Community College. I told him that the council selected appointees according to their location, not institutions. But that made no sense either as the area around Lorman had no representation. When I finally got him off the phone, I went immediately to Porter Fortune's office and told him that we had to do something. Walter came onto the council as an appointee of Governor Finch. Perhaps Porter had a conversation with the governor. Walter was a faithful supporter of the program and hosted meetings for me to meet with his faculty at any time I called.

I had no input into the council's membership, yet I always counted the number of women and blacks on the council. Once, after the appointment of new members, I informed the MHC of how many women were on the council, and Walter said, "Cora, you want all the members of the council to be women." He was a stalwart member, and I greatly appreciated his contributions. *Ebony* magazine cited Walter Washington for three consecutive years as one of the most influential black Americans. He was the first black student who received a Ph.D. from a Mississippi university.

Prior to leaving the council, J. O. Emmerich nominated Newton James from McComb and stated that he exemplified the story-telling tradition of the South. He also said, "Newt will inject humor and common sense into all discussions."

Robert Mayo

In the 1970s, the MHC adopted the policy that active members became advisory members of the council after serving their tenure and held advisory status forever. Robert Mayo, president of Hinds Community College, commented, "It's like the Mafia—once a member always a member." We found that our advisory members continued to be staunch advocates for our programs.

In 1976, Governor Bill Waller presented Chancellor Porter Fortune the Governor's Outstanding Mississippian Award

Porter Fortune and Governor Bill Waller

and emphasized Fortune's contributions to education as chairperson of the Mississippi Humanities Council and by his encouragement of an in-depth study of future needs of public education in the state. The MHC funded three Governor's Conferences on Education while Waller was governor.

Well aware of a growing perception that it was an adjunct of the University of Mississippi rather than a state-wide organization, the council owed John Bettersworth a debt of gratitude for taking Tad Thrash, director of Mississippi Institutions of Higher Learning, home for a lunch of turnip greens and corn bread while he visited MSU. Perhaps Tad's love for turnip greens made him offer space for our offices at the Research & Development Center in Jackson. In June 1977, the MHC office moved to the R & D Center.

While we were on its campus, the University of Mississippi received and dispersed our federal funds, but the Board of Institutions of Higher Learning rejected those responsibilities.

Savings and Loan Bank on Lynch Street in Jackson agreed to act as fiscal agent due to the efforts of Estus Smith.

Sadie Clark

At the same time we moved the office, Sadie Clark's husband, Dane Clark, graduated from law school, and she was unable to move with us. It saddened me, but I hosted a luncheon for Dane at my home following his graduation, and the council presented Sadie with a resolution upon her resignation. Although there were additional paragraphs, I included the following:

WHEREAS, she has treaded with care the bureaucratic maze of the University of Mississippi, has with honey-tongued telephone technique cultivated friends for the Committee throughout Mississippi (and, indeed the nation), and has accurately and efficiently maintained the Committee's books to the satisfaction, nay, to the utter delight of ferreting accountants and auditors.

WHEREAS, she has not only introduced many scholars in the humanities to the state-based program but has encouraged their participation, rousing the indolent, soothing the militant, solacing the disconsolate, and converting the hostile, and

WHEREAS, she has without reservation and with unquestionable competence served as the staff's token Black.

Porter Fortune

Even with his full schedule of events as Chancellor of Ole Miss, Porter Fortune never attempted to reschedule any appointment with me or any MHC activity; he always kept the original appointment. When I saw Porter off campus, I saw a different individual. On campus, he was THE CHANCELLOR, and few people felt as close to him as the members of the MHC who worked with him for several years. As I looked back, I decided it was the staff in the chancellor's office who caused one to enter with awe. I seldom saw Porter in his office and usually conducted my business with him off campus.

Porter Fortune died in September 1989. I wrote the following tribute and sent it to his wife Elizabeth and their children:

At Porter Fortune's funeral service we learned that his favorite Scripture was Micah 6:8, ". . . and what doth the Lord require of thee, but to do justly, and to love mercy, and to walk humbly with thou God?" Apparently these words struck a deep chord because he embodied them in his life as we observed him.

Mississippians are indebted to Porter Fortune for his leadership throughout the 1970s when we were experiencing much anguish with the desegregation of our society. As a university president he had a demanding schedule. However, he was often asked to be the spokesman for issues outside of higher education because of his dynamic public speaking ability. He spoke with conviction without a written text. Sometimes in preparation for a speech he would simply jot some notes around the edges of an envelope.

He never turned away from those highly controversial issues which he could easily have avoided because of his ongoing duties as chancellor of the University of Mississippi. No doubt, the tremendous stress year after year contributed to his health problems. Even when sick, public pressures allowed him little time for recuperation. Once following major surgery he was conducting summer commencement at Ole Miss within a matter of days.

Chancellor Fortune championed the freedom to express oneself and was instrumental in the Board of Institutions of Higher Learning refraining from censoring student newspapers at our public universities. During the early 1970s he also took on the chairmanship of the newly organized Mississippi Humanities Council to mount public humanities programs to discuss issues of human concern. In the early years all funded programs dealt with educational issues. And in 1972 the last thing school administrators wanted was yet another public meeting to talk about educational issues brought by the desegregation of public schools. Because Porter Fortune's name bestowed credibility to the highly suspect program funded with federal funds, I as staff person was able to move into communities and small towns throughout Mississippi and offer to the local citizens their first integrated public meeting. He was also recognized as a national leader in this unique program. At the first national meeting of state humanities programs held in Washington, D. C., in 1973, Porter Fortune was tapped to be a principal speaker. Today programs funded by the MHC enjoy a reputable image. When the American Association of University Women was pushing for public kindergartens, it was Porter Fortune who was asked to address a legislative group. He knew the controversy and risk involved. He was well aware that he would feel much heat from his higher education constituents. Even so, he delivered a forceful and persuasive speech to the legislative body and gained support which no doubt laid the groundwork for much of the Educational Reform Act of 1982.

In 1969-70 public schools were desegregated in Mississippi, and fears were rampant. Whites who certainly could ill afford the cost were seeking private schools for their children. I well remember a public meeting held in the Oxford High School the week before the school opened to blacks. The auditorium held a record number of parents who were fearful of the change which was upon them. The situation was tense. Porter Fortune stepped to the podium and reiterated his belief in and support of public education. He allayed many fears that night when he calmly said, "Come Monday morning my children will be in Oxford Public High School."

His sincerity, his good common sense, and his humor endeared him to all who had the privilege to work with him. In the midst of controversy Porter could inject humor—his trademark. Displaying humility, he often made himself the butt of his stories.

Our lives have been enriched because Porter L. Fortune stretched his daily schedule many, many times to make room for one more trip, one more meeting, one more speech. We were especially pleased when we could claim him for a party. He made his time count. Lib Fortune and her children shared this man with Mississippians. Lib's house must be painfully empty today. In the years ahead, may warm memories drive the sadness away.

At the Tenth Anniversary Conference in 1982, Porter Fortune gave his summation of life: "A good life demands that one have something to work for, something to hope for, and someone to love."

Estus Smith, Chair: 1977-1982

Estus Smith

Estus Smith became chair of the Mississippi Humanities Council in 1977 and served in that capacity for the next five years. He was active in the council's work from the beginning and attended many of its programs. He did much that strengthened the programs and presented a united council to the public. Estus believed a proposal funded without a unanimous vote needed to be revised until ALL council members were pleased and left the meeting saying, "WE funded that proposal." He knew it was easy to turn down a proposal, but if the concerned group sincerely wanted a public humanities program, he stated, "We'll work with them until their proposal meets MHC's guidelines."

The council interviewed Dennis Mitchell, an Ole Miss graduate in history, while we were still on the Ole Miss campus. They hired him as our assistant director of MHC, and he began work in the Jackson office. A better choice was impossible. Dennis was a wonderful person with whom to work, and he usually began my day with an interesting tidbit of history, such as "Where did we get the 'Irish' potato?" Ireland, of course! No, it came from South America.

Dennis Mitchell

Dennis was open to all people, never objected to traveling, and gave me tremendous support. He paved the way for our scholar-in-residence, Joe Stockwell from the English Department at Mississippi State University, to serve in Waynesboro. Dennis talked with the newspaper publisher, the Board of Supervisors, and the librarian. He sold the board on the idea, and the librarian provided space for Stockwell. Although Dennis left us after three years and accepted a teaching position at Jackson State University, he continued his involvement in the humanities program and spoke to library audiences and civic organizations. In

2008, he received the MHC's Chair's Award for Special Achievements in the Humanities.

Joe Stockwell spent several weeks as our scholar-in-residence in Waynesboro but had a quite different experience than O. F. White, our scholar-in-residence in Greenville at that same time. Dr. White, recently retired from Delta State University, had a thorny start, but Imogene Borganelli, a council member from Greenville, stepped in and saw that he had invitations to speak at almost every civic club there. Dr. Stockwell, housed at the library in Waynesboro, had few contacts with civic organizations, but the local newspaper finally asked him to write a weekly column. His last column noted that some young boys brought their little red wagon to the library and loaded it with books to take home. Joe commented, "As long as little boys load their red wagons with books, I know that I shall have a job at Mississippi State University." Because he had no local sponsorship and was, therefore, at a disadvantage, I thought his time in Waynesboro demanded recognition. I wrote Joe Duffey, chairman at NEH, and requested a letter of thanks to the president of Mississippi State University for Joe's participation in our new program. Duffey asked for a draft of a letter for him to send; I provided it. Then I heard from Stockwell . . . "What a hell of a time for me to get a letter from the chairman of the National Endowment of the Humanities when I had just been raked over the coals for spending my time in Waynesboro when I should have been doing research!"

The scholars-in-residence programs touched several communities in which we had few regular programs. Seena Kohn, a sociologist, spent several months in Neshoba County and examined the relations between the three cultures there—the whites, blacks, and Choctaws. A folklorist explored the culture of Yazoo County, and in Madison County, a scholar explored and recorded the impact of urbanization on a traditionally rural community. In Tupelo, an archaeologist worked on a project with the artifacts of the Chickasaw culture.

With NEH award money, we sponsored a program in DeSoto County, where George B. Crawford, an historian, generated so much interest in local history that the community formed a foundation for further support. Lawrence J. Nelson, also an historian, encouraged Pearl River County citizens to increase awareness of their own heritage.

Other scholars-in-residence programs included Page Guttierrez, who made Biloxi city government officials aware of the impact of a scholar's field work in their city and aided in the establishment of a seafood museum. We also had philosophers as ethicists-in-residence in two hospitals: Wallace Murphree, philosopher at Mississippi State University, at St. Dominic Hospital in Jackson and Tom Flynn, philosopher at the University of Mississippi, at the North Mississippi Medical Center in Tupelo.

I owed Estus Smith, already chairperson, much gratitude for the moral support he gave me during a discrimination case filed after I fired a secretary. Soon after the office moved to Jackson in 1977, I found myself in a situation that could have ended my career if council members had not backed me completely with their confidence and trust. After we moved, I hired a new secretary because my administrative assistant Sadie Clark resigned when we left Ole Miss. The young woman I hired was most attractive and competent.

I left the office early one afternoon for a beauty parlor appointment and left some typing for the secretary to finish. I apparently irked her for going during working hours. However, during those early years, I worked almost every weekend—especially Sundays—with MHC programs. I received no compensation for overtime and had no qualms about a beauty parlor appointment during working hours. When I returned before 5 p.m., the work I gave the secretary was on my desk with the note, "You can type these." I went to her desk and fired her on the spot. I then called the maintenance people, had our office door locks changed that afternoon, and reported the situation to Estus. He asked council members Sarah Rouse and Roy Thigpen to meet at my office that evening. When I related the details to those three, they all supported my actions.

I soon received a notice to appear before the Equal Employment Opportunity Commission (EEOC). I was alone when I got to the EEOC office, but shortly afterward, Estus appeared by my side. I remain grateful to him. At that time, he was vice president of Jackson State University, and it was registration day on his campus. But he stayed with me throughout the ordeal and showed his support when he also had pressing duties at the university. After that meeting with the personnel at EEOC, I never had further communication with their office.

As I looked back on the staff members employed during my tenure, I knew I had the most complete support from Brenda Gray in all aspects of my job. She joined the staff in 1979 after receiving her bachelor's degree at Jackson State University and quickly received a promotion to administrative secretary. In 1983 Brenda became an administrative assistant and was

Brenda Gray

responsible for organizing the office work and handling regrant financial reports.

In 1988, I reported to the council that Brenda would complete the bookkeeping in-house and prepare all financial reports to NEH instead of the certified public accountant. In 1991 she received her master's degree in business education at JSU. Brenda continues her work with the MHC, and I value her support and friendship through the years.

Soon after moving to Jackson, I met Boyd Golding, who worked in the Mississippi State University office at the R & D Center. He became a personal friend. We utilized some of our funds to hire retired persons— Ruby Thompson, Barbara Carroon, and Boyd Golding, who all worked far more hours than they submitted for payment. We were all indebted for their support. Boyd loved parties and helped me with every get-together I had in my Jackson condo for over 20 years. Long involved with state politics and a former state auditor, he continually entertained our guests with one story after another.

Boyd Golding

One day Boyd and I hosted three parties. We always celebrated staff birthdays and did so that morning. At noon we hosted a luncheon for a new continuing education leader at Mississippi State University and then drove to Greenville, Mississippi, where I held a pre-wedding reception for Sanci Borganelli, Santo and Imogene Borganelli's daughter, and her fiancé Tom Ledwidge. For the party I reserved a small house, where we set up two bars. Boyd tended one of them and attracted most of the guests because of his gregarious personality. We returned to Jackson in the wee hours of the morning with a few new stories. When Boyd remarried and moved to Benton, Mississippi, I was jealous of Ramona for taking him away from Jackson and my parties.

While Joseph Duffey was chairman of NEH (1977-1981), I became rather brazen and called his office for an appointment. After several years of traveling the roads and byways in Mississippi promoting humanities programs, I wanted to meet the top VIP. When his office refused to make an appointment for me because of his pressing schedule, I immediately called Frank Barber in Senator Eastland's office and asked him to arrange a time for Duffey to have a drink with me. By that time, I knew that the congressional offices, especially those of the senators, had more influence on NEH than those of us in the heartland. In a few minutes, Frank called back and said, "Joe Duffey can't have a drink with you because he's going out of town, but he can have lunch with you." That was too much time! However, Frank agreed to go with us. I arrived at Duffey's office early and had to wait for him. In a few minutes, Barber appeared. When I told him we had to wait, he left immediately to dismiss the senator's limousine and driver. He no sooner returned than Duffey saw him and ran out to greet us.

I was delighted when Joe later came to Mississippi and met with several members of the MHC at a luncheon meeting in

Greenville that Imogene Borganelli arranged for us. As he sat on the banks of the Mississippi River, his wife, a member of President Carter's staff, was being wined and dined in Europe.

Estus, elected in 1975, was the first black to serve on the Board of Trustees, Mississippi Department of Archives and History. He testified before congressional hearings in 1977 and again in 1979 for the humanities' appropriations. After one such occasion, *The Washington Post* quoted him—quite an accolade for a Mississippian.

In 1977, Ernst and Ernst conducted our first management study. As I came via the sciences, chemistry and physics, I had no idea of what such a study encompassed. I was thankful for George Godwin and his leadership. That study helped us tremendously in assuring that we were always accountable for federal funds, and at the end of the study, the MHC presented George a plaque for guiding us through it.

Robert E. Bergmark taught philosophy at Millsaps College and was involved in many of our regrant programs. When I first approached Robert to participate, he replied, "It will take me months to prepare for such participation." He finally realized that he completed his months of preparation much earlier in his career. When we had a few programs on the role of technology in our society, Robert prepared a paper on "Computers and Persons." With more and more jobs in today's world dependent upon computers and increasing numbers of students in our colleges studying technology, the humanities are even more important today. We all should know that the end result of computer technology impacts society.

Bergmarks's paper took us back to fifth century B.C. Greece to the discrepancies between Democritus and his contemporary Socrates. Bergmark contended that Democritus gave us the foundation for all future science and technology, but Socrates laid the foundation for all future humanistic belief. I feel confident that his paper is even more pertinent to our society than when he wrote it:

> We are much impressed these days with what computers "say." . . . Computers do not "say"— they compute. With an ability to move through computations at the speed of light, the computer has enabled us to accomplish some amazing feats. But the computer must be programmed by a mind that is: (1) able to imagine the goal that is to be reached, (2) able to see how the computations can help reach that goal, and (3) able to develop the appropriate program for the computer to follow. Then, and only then, can a computer "say" anything, and that hardly qualifies as "saying." Computers are not persons. Computers are tools that persons use. . . . It is not involved with meanings, purposes, and values in the sense in which persons are. . . . The problem we face is the age-old problem of developing a society in which personal character will be nurtured and supported.

We appreciated Bob Bergmark's contributions to several of our programs and his support of my efforts on the Millsaps campus in the early days of the program.

Shortly after moving to the R & D Center, Harrylyn Sallis, who taught at Belhaven College in Jackson, visited me. She headed a program that encouraged mature women to get back into academe and knew that I had a late start with my professional life. She asked me to speak to a group at the college; of course I agreed. She soon returned, said there was criticism of my speaking on campus, and felt it was not a good idea. That was during our fight for the Equal Rights Amendment, and I was an adamant voice for its passage. I assured Harrylyn that it was entirely up to her. Then, Frances Mills, my long-time AAUW friend and a great supporter and former dean of Belhaven College, championed my participation in the program. She talked to the president. He agreed to attend my presentation and to then make himself available to anyone who complained. I spoke, and, to my knowledge, there were no complaints.

Harrylyn's husband Charles taught history at Millsaps College in Jackson. He, too, was involved in the state-based program and became a member of the council after my retirement. They made a great team.

Our liaisons at the National Endowment constantly confronted us about the humanities content of our regrant programs, and it was always a concern of council members and mine as we made each regrant. When NEH sent someone to evaluate our regrant to Central Mississippi, Inc., an early Head Start program, I was completely unaware of it until I received their negative evaluation. I wrote NEH in response and stated it needed to be part of the evaluation record that the organization held those programs in the courthouses of Attala, Carroll, Grenada, and Montgomery counties— counties located in Central Mississippi, an area where public, integrated meetings were the exception and not the rule. The evaluation reports submitted by the project director as well as the outside evaluator failed to include the following points, which further validated the programs and increased their significance: (a) the organization was predominantly black,

(b) the programs were in county courthouses where white mayors welcomed attendees, (c) the panels consisted of scholars in the humanities from institutions of higher learning throughout the state and white elected representatives, and (d) the issues concerned recession, energy crises, and the desegregation of public schools in Mississippi—all public policy issues. Although the recorded attendance was small, the fact that such meetings even occurred in Winona, Grenada, Kosciusko, and Carrollton said something in Mississippi at that time. I further added that the regrant we made to Central Mississippi, Inc., was for eight programs, but without any increase in funds, they actually coordinated and administered twelve programs.

Michael Harrington, who participated in programs from the very first and knew of the criticism from NEH, wrote me a letter concerning this matter. The following was only a portion of Michael's letter:

> . . . During the past three years I have participated in more than fifty such programs, and labored annually in workshops for scholars in the humanities as well as evaluation conferences attempting to determine how effectively the humanities were being brought to bear on public policy issues. I have also served as a community consultant, helping to write more than a dozen program proposals, and worked as project director for several funded grants. Accordingly, I can speak from both personal and professional experience as to just how well the humanities have been involved in programs sponsored by the state-based committee. . . . Therefore, I submit that this charge is false. . .

Perhaps Michael's letter said more in our defense than I was able to say at the time.

Peyton Williams, at the August 1978 meeting of the council, proposed broadening the guidelines for funded programs by incorporating issues ". . . of human concern . . . which direct attention to the basic values and assumptions of human beings in society." He felt all programs should not have to directly relate public policy issues and a governmental solution but could "involve cultural enrichment through activities designed to contribute to the broadening of understanding of cultural ideas by the general public, primarily through discourse with professionals in the humanities." He went on to say that exhibits, media displays, and other prepared materials could be used "as aids to discourse" but could not take the place of a panel discussion. His guidelines were adopted by the council.

In 1977 or 1978, Peyton stepped up to help me with a program funded in Greenville. The community planned an evening with writers from the Mississippi Delta who had earned national recognition, including Walker Percy and Shelby Foote. To show appreciation for their funding, the project director asked me to introduce the writers that evening. Having never read one book authored by these august writers, I called Peyton, a literature scholar. He said, "Cora, accept their invitation; I'll write an introduction for you." He did, and I was most grateful. He saved my reputation and especially that of the council.

In 1978, University of Southern Mississippi held a two-day symposium "Sense of Place" on the campus at Hattiesburg to identify and discuss the distinctive attributes of Mississippi, its land, its people, and its culture. A specific goal was the exploration of factors which contributed to the development of a Mississippian's sense of place. In addition, the symposium participants identified the individual and community values arising from a strong sense of place and examined the policies and actions of the media, governmental agencies, and businesses that promoted or threatened a citizen's bond with his or her environment. In 1979, USM learned that the symposium received a national award, the 1979 Creative Programming Award, an annual award from the Conferences Institutes Executive Committee of the National University Extension Association.

We gave a mini-grant, no more than $1000, to H. T. Sampson Library at Jackson State University for "Gowdy: Cherishing This Heritage" that examined the sense of place of the residents of the small community of Gowdy, Mississippi. It created a unique moment in the lives of the audience and shed light on the unique Mississippi sense of community. It was, perhaps, the best project in terms of audience development that the evaluator ever attended.

Imogene Borganelli

I was delighted when the council elected Imogene Borganelli, my long-time friend, to its membership in 1978. I kept her apprised of the council's activities from the beginning and knew she was a strong advocate for the council and for me personally. We first met at a statewide meeting of the American Association of University Women in

Jackson, Mississippi, in the mid-sixties. The second night of the conference we found ourselves without roommates and decided to share a room. I helped Imogene move her things into my room. For that one weekend conference, she had at least seven pairs of shoes and seven purses to match! We continued to get together at meetings of AAUW, and it was a friendship that blossomed with each meeting.

As AAUW members, we supported a Status of Women's Commission in Mississippi. A group of women in Jackson met for lunch at a hotel restaurant prior to a meeting with Governor Finch to lobby for the commission. Imogene and I decided to ride with Dr. Melerson Guy Dunham, whose car was in the parking lot of the hotel. When we reached the car, we found that Dr. Dunham's driver was a young black girl and that they had the back seat filled with items for the museum at Prentiss Institute—plows, hoes, and other farm equipment. We moved plows and harnesses and finally made room for the two of us to sit in the back seat. The young woman backed out and somehow locked the back bumper onto the back bumper of the car parked next to us. Imogene and I were scared that we were in trouble with the owner of that car. Imogene, in high heels and white gloves, got up on the back bumper and jumped up and down to unlock the two bumpers. When we saw a white man coming toward us, our hearts sank! He looked over the situation without any show of malice and suggested that he get into his car and back it out at the same time the young driver backed Dr. Dunham's car. It worked. We got to the governor's office with our high heels and white gloves slightly greased!

Jane Crater Hiatt and I became very close friends while she directed the Tennessee program, and I sought advice from her many times after she and her husband moved to the

Mississippi Gulf Coast. In 1981, the council hired Jane as our assistant director. Peyton Williams, a member of the Search Committee, said to me after they made the selection, "I don't want to come to Jackson and find you two estranged." I think Peyton was far wiser than I knew at that time.

Jane assisted proposal writers in their efforts and won their admiration and respect in the process. She guided the implementation of the Chairman's Award for the Scholar-in-Residence Program through public recognition of its success. Her exuberance, energy, intellect, and experience contributed immeasurably to furthering public programs in the humanities in Mississippi.

Jane was far better than I in many aspects of administration, but I maintained control of the budget and never exceeded it during my 24 years of working with federal funds. I was aware that Jane wanted control of the budget when she worked with a program, and we lost the closeness we once had, a point that troubled me greatly. In 1985, while on sabbatical in England, I received a message that she accepted the executive director's position with the Jackson/Hinds County Arts Alliance.

In 1977, we had an organizational meeting for the Federation of State Humanities Councils in Minneapolis. The Mississippi council nominated Estus Smith to serve on the federation's board of directors. Martin Schwartz from Indiana presided at the opening session, officers were chosen, and Estus was elected to that first board. Those elected drew lots for their terms of office, but Estus had to leave the meeting before that was done; I drew for him—a one-year term. Schwartz was one of the early persons contacted by NEH for the formation of a federation, and we thought he would make an exceptional president of the board. He was not chosen but remained active and visited us in Mississippi in 1980. Later, the federation offered a Martin Schwartz Prize for the best public program presented by a state council. We also learned to appreciate Bernard O'Kelly, who became the first president.

At the end of Estus' first year on the board of directors, the Mississippi council wanted to nominate him for a second term, but he said his responsibilities at Jackson State University were too consuming. The council nominated Imogene Borganelli. Then, at the federation's meeting in Albuquerque, New Mexico, my AAUW friend, Jean Walz from South Dakota, nominated Estus. Since each state could only nominate one person, Jean's nomination of a Mississippian spoke loudly of the respect and admiration he claimed on the first board of the federation. Imogene quickly withdrew her name, and Estus was elected for a second term.

At the federation meeting in Baltimore in 1981, Estus presided at the evening banquet; Jane Hiatt conducted a session on program participants, and Hazel Portwood and I served as social organizers with an open bar in our room. Mississippi was truly spotlighted. At such meetings, I always stayed up late holding forth at the bar and visiting with other executive directors across the nation. In Baltimore, Hazel and I shared a room. When I returned to our room in the wee hours of the night, Hazel was in bed asleep, but she always left the TV blazing so that I would not disturb her when I returned. I am indebted to Hazel for her many notes since my retirement urging me to finish this book.

I included the background of the Federation of State Humanities Councils because Mississippi's council was an integral entity in that organization from its formation. Our council members continue to be elected to its board, and today (2009), Willis Lott, president of the Mississippi Gulf Coast Community College, serves as president of the federation.

Initially, only council members were eligible to serve on the federation's board of directors. The by-laws changed after a few years and executive directors were also eligible to serve, but I never sought a position. I thought my non-paid council members carried far more weight with the congressional delegation than I, a paid worker.

In the early days of the federation, the Tennessee Humanities Council decided not to join and simply refused to pay their dues. The board sent Estus Smith to Tennessee to convince them that all states were needed to make the federation's program effective. Returning from Tennessee, Estus sent me the following letter:

> It is good to see another State Humanities Committee in action. We should thank our dear God for you. I knew you were valuable, but it took my Nashville experience to assess your true value.

> Among other things, several members of the KKK shared a flight with me from Memphis to Nashville. We could have shared a limousine to the hotel. However, since they had made it known to everybody in our section of the plane, I did not deem it wise to share a cab with the unmasked men.

> There isn't anything dull in working for the Mississippi Committee for the Humanities.

Later, I nominated Tennessee's executive director Robert Cheatham for the presidency of the federation's board of directors; he was elected.

The first executive director of the federation, elected by the board of directors, was Steve Weiland, who deserved much of the credit for the early successes. In 1985, the council invited him to Mississippi to help us with our long-range planning meeting. I found that the Federation of State Humanities Councils not only proved to be a strong voice in lobbying in Washington for all the councils but also gave us the opportunity to make new friends across the nation during annual meetings. I value those friendships today, and although I lost contact with many during the years that I cared for my mother, I kept up with some.

I was a strong proponent of networking while I worked in the state humanities program and carried a list of outstanding speakers with me at all times. If someone asked for a recommendation for a speaker, I usually had one to offer.

In the late 1970s, some professors at Jackson State University—Robert Smith, Bill Cooley, and Oscar Rogers—planned "An Evening with Estus Smith." His colleagues; friends; council members; Gary Messinger, who represented NEH; Dr. Bernard O'Kelly, the president of the board of the newly formed Federation of State Humanities Councils; and his administrative assistant Ellen Erickson, both from The University of North Dakota, attended. I spoke to the large audience for the MHC:

> It is a special honor to be the spokesperson for the Mississippi Humanities Council, because with Dr. Smith around, I don't get the opportunity very often.

Although I must admit when it really hit me what
this evening is all about, I knew that this role was
completely out of character for me. I am not known
for singing public praises of males and certainly not
of black males who are the most chauvinistic of all!
Therefore, Dr. Smith, I shall stick strictly to facts.
It is fact that the state humanities program launched
in Mississippi in 1972 has claimed more of your
time than of any other citizen in Mississippi outside
the paid staff, and you've been known to question
that statement. I well remember the day I first met
you—you won't let me forget it—my first time to
truly experience the state of being a minority . . . As
I plunged into black communities, you were there;
for the first program on the Choctaw reservation, you
were there; if the program dealt with a controversial
issue, you were there.

You have represented the Mississippi council in
regional and national meetings. You have been sought
by other states as they have grappled with their own
humanities programs. Indeed, such exposure has on
several occasions brought to you attractive offers to
leave Mississippi.

You epitomize what education is all about—the
ability to think straight (why hell, high water, nor a
governor from Mississippi can bring pressure upon
you to change your stand), a knowledge of the past
with vision for the future, skills to do useful service,
and a commitment to the well-being of the community.
You surely must hold the record for sitting on
boards, committees, commissions, councils—why
you've even served on the Executive Board of the

Girl Scouts. Some of these board members are here tonight. In fact, we are all here tonight to attest to the fact that you have not merely held membership in our organizations, but you have been a leader and contributed to a better program for each one of them.

We would all recall some words of Martin Luther King. "I have a dream that one day . . . even the State of Mississippi, a state sweltering with the heat of injustice, sweltering with the heat of oppression, will be transformed into an oasis of freedom and justice."

We may not yet have the oasis of freedom and justice, but we sit together tonight at the table of personhood, and you can take no little pride in the fact that you have contributed to the realization of Martin Luther King's dream for Mississippi

Now, lest you think that you are going to rest upon your laurels, we've news for you tonight! We would hasten to remind you, Dr. Smith, that we did not go to all this trouble tonight to pay homage to a "has been" but rather to show you our support for your now launching an even more active and rigorous participation in the affairs of this state. You have shown us your talents, so we expect MUCH more from you! Enjoy your glory tonight. It is richly deserved. But, come Monday morning, I hope that you will forget all the flattering speeches as some of us have still got to work with you, and we pray that you will continue to be the man of equanimity, of magnanimity, of humility which ALL of us have recognized and for which the acclaim is yours tonight. Estus, even a feminist readily admits tonight that you

have prevailed to bring recognized leadership to all
of us.

Bernard O'Kelly and Ellen Erickson returned to North
Dakota, and in a few days, I received the following letter
signed by each:

> We learned much from you about the validity of the
> name Hospitality State . . . The testimonial dinner for
> Estus went splendidly in every respect . . . Having
> seen you in action on your own turf, we understand
> why the MHC has had such a success record. You
> are not just efficient, informed, thoughtful, clear-
> minded, and decisive, but downright assertive, too,
> and people like it. Thanks for exerting the necessary
> pressure to make sure the Federation of State
> Humanities Councils was represented.

At the November 1979 meeting of the MHC, Estus Smith,
chair, welcomed the council members to the meeting held
in the President's Dining Room at Jackson State University.
He presented the following evaluation of the program at that
time:

> It is difficult to believe that less than ten years ago
> there was no real public interest in the humanities
> in the state of Mississippi. . . .What was truly
> discouraging was that there did not seem to be
> the slightest interest in search for answers to the
> problems of war and peace, oppression, starvation,
> racial inequality, and inhumanity in general which
> have plagued this planet since the beginning of time.
> . . Then, as if by magic, in 1971, five Mississippians
> were invited to visit the National Endowment for

the Humanities in Washington. I represented Dr.
Peoples, who was invited to that meeting. Dr. Cora
Norman was subsequently appointed director of the
Mississippi Committee for the Humanities, and the
pendulum began to swing in the other direction for
Mississippians. The Mississippi Committee for the
Humanities has insisted that the people of this state
confront some of the most basic problems of the state
and nation. This committee has helped scholars in
the humanities regain faith in themselves and their
work. This committee has helped this state regain
faith in itself. . . . The Mississippi Committee for the
Humanities has made a significant impact on the lives
of many Americans. You have sought to get projects
funded into every county in the state of Mississippi
with the hope that the concept would reach out and
touch any and all persons of the state. We must
continue our commitment to programs of public
policy issues. We must continue our commitment
to grass roots level programs. . . . We must use the
Mississippi Committee for the Humanities' model
to see that all segments of society are involved. It
is out of desperation that the essence of this charge
comes. Our society needs to enlist the talents, skills,
special knowledge, and experiences of the scholars
in the humanities. If the basic problems in human
relations are to be resolved, the experience of the
historian is needed to assay the potholes and pitfalls
that have aggravated mankind in the past. The faith
of the theologian is needed. The value judgment of
the philosopher and precision of the legal scholar are
needed in the battle for a better world.

Then in 1980, Peyton Williams told us how to introduce the humanities:

> The humanities did not begin in Congress . . . [but] took their name from Cicero's humanitas and are the disciplined embodiments of humanism. . . . Historically, it began the reaction against that medieval extremism which diminished the whole human being. . . . The humanities are set apart and unified in dedication to upholding and enhancing the dignity, the worth, and the wholeness of human beings. . . . The key is the respectful sharing aimed at growth in understanding and stature as persons . . . and hence, incidentally, as citizens.

At that meeting, Bill Scaggs, president of Meridian Community College, pleaded for "activities which speak to the universality of the human experience . . . . Activities which highlight the values of the human experience are the essence of what MHC programs should encompass." He evaluated what the MHC should do:

> Use grassroots sources when funds are limited, then spend on leadership which would serve as a ripple effect on all humanity. "Sense of Place" is an example of a way to achieve this; it gave leaders an opportunity to come together and focus on an issue. Use media more effectively. . . . People in professional education have broader concerns than educating for skills but are unable to turn opinion around without help since public institutions cannot do much more than the public encourages. My highest aspiration is that the humanities will be a vehicle which emphasizes those values that unite us as human beings."

Roy Hudson, Mississippi Valley State University, reported for the fund raising committee in 1981, and reminded the council once again of its commitment to a public humanities program:

> State humanities programs were funded on the supposition that democracy demands wisdom and vision in its citizens, and the world leadership which has come to the U. S. cannot rest solely upon superior power, wealth, and technology but must be solidly founded upon worldwide respect and admiration for the nation's high qualities as a leader in the realm of ideas and of the spirit. Our scholars in the humanities must not forget, and must not let us forget, our primary responsibility in the molding of future citizens for a democracy. Our programs have exposed citizens to ideas and concepts to which they might otherwise not have been exposed. Horizons have been broadened. Race relations improved.

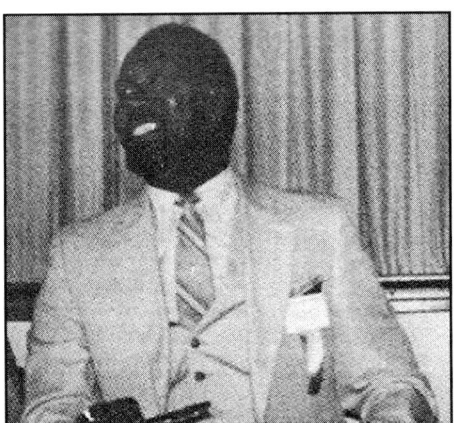

Roy Hudson

Roy's overriding conviction was "a vision for Mississippi must evolve from this state—not borrow from other states."

One of my experiences with Roy was quite memorable even though the issue involved was not. He brought a bus load of students from his campus to the R & D Center in Jackson to talk to Ted Thrash, director of Institutions of Higher Learning. Whatever the issue, Ted had no appointment to talk with the students, and the security people closely kept their eyes on the group. When I looked out our office window and saw Roy in the courtyard with the students, I immediately went down to talk with him. When I got to the door leading outside to the courtyard, the security guards stopped me, not wanting me to meet with the group. Insisting, I went out and gave Roy a hug and a kiss. Thrash finally agreed to talk with a few of the students, and afterward they peacefully returned to their bus and headed back to their campus at Itta Bena. I remembered my student days and knew that as long as there have been campuses, students have occasionally rebelled against issues. It is much more productive to talk with them than to turn one's back on their questions. I kept up with Roy through the years and knew that he served as president of MVSU until recently.

I often said that the best humanities programs were those that were initially controversial and required much discussion amongst the council members before being funded. However, this reached its climax in the early 1980s. For some time during the discussion of whether or not a proposal should be funded, Newton James, a McComb businessman and future mayor, and Constance Slaughter-Harvey, a lawyer working in state government, expressed opposing views. Both were much involved in the state-based program, and both were recognized leaders.

Newton James carried all the attributes of a southern white conservative but was a confidant and close friend of Oliver Emmerich, editor of the McComb newspaper. Emmerich stood for the rights of all citizens, and the Ku Klux Klan in McComb retaliated by having many of its members cancel their newspaper subscriptions. Although many perceived Newton as a conservative, he shared Emmerich's stand on civil rights. He told me when race relations were really tense in McComb, he and Oliver often had their conversations in the car to ensure privacy.

I knew Newton and appreciated what he contributed to the humanities program, but an earlier incident demonstrated that he was not the typical, white conservative businessman. Weeks after Brenda Gray joined the MHC as secretary, we were at a council meeting at the downtown Holiday Inn, now known as the Marriott. She cashed her first monthly paycheck and had the money in her purse. Someone stole it, and Brenda was in tears. I knew that I could not write another check, but Newton pulled out his personal checkbook and wrote Brenda a check for the amount stolen from her.

In 1970, Constance Slaughter-Harvey was the first black woman to graduate from the University of Mississippi School of Law. She was also a graduate of Tougaloo College and much involved in civil rights activities throughout her years there. As one of the early black students at Ole Miss, she faced many obstacles and earned her right to stand up and ask questions. Constance was involved in the humanities program for several years and was the project director of a number of regrants held in rural areas of the state. She made sure that the humanities professors she selected delivered for the programs. Once, when she was unhappy with a professor's performance, she refused to pay him. When he returned for the second program, he performed much more suitably.

When Constance joined the council, she was determined that all proposals involving blacks would get a fair evaluation. Such was always true of the council's funding, but she was unaware of that.

Some long forgotten issue sent Newt into orbit during one particular council meeting. At previous meetings, he quietly

Constance
Slaughter-Harvey

tolerated remarks from Constance, but that day he was not in the mood to answer her questions. He stood up, shredded the proposals in front of him, and said, "I don't have to take this. I need to be back in my business in McComb." Obviously, the meeting was short lived after that outburst. The fact that Gary Messinger, our liaison from NEH, happened to be there that day added to the awkwardness of the situation. On her way out, Constance said to me, "I'll resign." Because I knew her well and was much indebted to her for all her work with humanities programs, I said, "You can't. You started this, and you've got to see it through." Constance missed the next meeting but then returned to complete her term. Newton also returned for subsequent council meetings.

Peyton Williams, on the Screening Committee for evaluating proposals, immediately wrote a letter to Constance that conveyed his distress over the situation and in which he took responsibility "for not making fuller notes in the subcommittee session" the day before. He expressed his gratitude for the increased participation by the entire council in debating and choosing regrants and pointed out that Connie had a large part in making that happen. He closed the letter by hoping that tensions could be "put behind us, for the sake of the program and the people of Mississippi." Peyton's letter showed how he valued the public humanities program and how important he felt it was for the council members to voice conflicting opinions.

The saga continued. The Office of the Secretary of State had a position open and had an applicant from McComb. Constance, already employed there, picked up the phone and called her former adversary, Newton James, for his recommendation!

The saga deepened. Newton served his term as mayor of McComb and retired. The Board of Supervisors hosted a dinner honoring one of its own and asked Constance to speak, lauding the person's tenure with the board. Later, I heard that when she got up to speak, she saw Newton James in the audience and acknowledged him with complimentary remarks.

Cora Norman and Newton James

Connie and Newt remained close friends. I relied on both of them as we worked to promote the humanities program in Mississippi. Today, we can laugh at the episode above and appreciate each other even more. I usually talk with Newt on his birthday, and he is always upbeat and ready to tell me a story. I also keep up with Constance. In 2006, she received the W.E.B. DuBois Award from a group in Jackson and later a Margaret Brent Award in Honolulu from the Commission on Women of the American Bar Association. In 2008, she delivered an address at Vanderbilt Law School in remembrance of Martin Luther King.

Left to right: Constance Slaughter-Harvey and Lenore Prather.

I related this story because it epitomized what we tried to do in the early days of the program. Both Newton James and Constance Slaughter-Harvey gave me permission to include it. When I wrote to request permission from him, Newt replied:

> Constance Slaughter-Harvey was intelligent, well educated, had ideas and convictions, and she had the courage to express them in public and fight for them,

too! I admire her for that. She and I agreed on most
projects and programs, but we did have some heated
exchanges in a few board meetings.

It was quite a challenge at that time to bring black and white
leaders together to express themselves in a public meeting.
We maintained that people could disagree, state their points
of view, leave the meeting having expressed their feelings,
and still respect those persons with whom they disagreed. We
got black and white leaders to discuss issues, but there were
certainly few times when they expressed any disagreement.
When such occurred, there was simply silence. It was the
silence that devastated us. We needed more forums in which
the group could express and discuss different ideas, bringing
the community closer together instead of isolating certain
members. When people do not express their opinions,
they are left out of the discussion of the issue. Susan A.
Cole, president of Metropolitan State University, St. Paul,
Minnesota, addressed this lack of conversation in our society
at the annual meeting of the American Council on Education
in 1995.

Because of the kindness Carole Huxley and Len Oliver
demonstrated after my volatile initial visit with John
Barcroft, I forever felt that the NEH staff was always ready
to offer me help and advice when needed. Near the end of my
tenure with the state-based program, I was well aware that
some of the states' executive directors were at odds with the
staff at NEH, and their attitudes reflected that at several of
the national meetings of executive directors. I never shared
their perspective of the NEH role. Our council had a close
relationship with B. J. Stiles, Division of State Programs,
who visited Mississippi several times. His last visit was just

prior to his resignation from NEH to take a position with the Council on Foundations; he sent the following letter:

> Although I hope to never disengage completely from either NEH or state programs, I can't approach my final day at work without sending a special thank you to you. From the outset, I have felt your personal good wishes and your professional support as I tried to sort out the priorities for this era. I could not have persisted without that support, and I am indebted to you for standing forward among the "old guard" to express support for shifting directions. . . . Thank you again for making a "final" visit possible in the late spring. Technically, it was the last trip I made on behalf of the Division, and I'm pleased that it was to be in Mississippi, and to talk about the future.

During my tenure with the Mississippi council, I really had few contacts with the chairs at NEH. Bill Bennett, chairperson 1982-1985, was a professor at University of Southern Mississippi, but I met him when he headed up the National Humanities Center in North Carolina. In fact, I sat in his office in North Carolina in March 1981 and listened to the radio with him the day John Hinckley, Jr. shot President Reagan. When the President was ready to nominate a chairperson for the National Endowment for the Humanities, I felt Bill was a good choice and discussed it with Peyton Williams, who contacted Senator Stennis and lobbied for Bennett.

In a proposal which I later submitted to NEH, I used the word *excellent* to describe some of MHC's programs. It came back to me to define the term. I firmly believed that we had some excellent programs in Mississippi, but I also knew that those same programs would not have met the criteria for excellence in Massachusetts, a much more sophisticated state. When word got around to the executive directors that Cora had to define excellent for Bill Bennett, my Georgia colleague Ron Benson sent me this quote from G. E. Moore, a well known philosopher: "What's good is good, and that's all there is to it." I sent it to Bennett and heard no more from him; it possibly saved my reputation.

There were times during Bennett's administration when I believed he thought he was the ONLY scholar capable of addressing public policy issues. Later he came to Mississippi to speak at MSU and then joined us for a reception held for him at what was then the downtown Deposit and Guaranty Bank Building.

However, while Bill Bennett was chair of the NEH, the MHC was one of five state councils that received the National Endowment Chairman's Award for Excellence. The picture below captured Bennett's presentation of the award to me in Washington, D. C. After returning to Mississippi, I awaited a copy of the picture to publicize the award.

Cora Norman and Bill Bennett

Finally I called, and NEH responded with at least a hundred copies!

In 1982, Estus Smith appointed a planning committee of Charles Dunagin, chairman; Mary Benjamin; John Guice; William S. Haynie; Charles V. McTeer; and Hazel Portwood to make arrangements for the council's tenth anniversary celebration. There was much discussion as to what we had accomplished. We were most fortunate to have an intern, Patricia Stevens, who served as coordinator for the program. Having lived in Jackson for years, she knew many of the community leaders and attracted people who were never involved prior to that conference.

Estus Smith and Patricia Stevens

The conference brought together not only our new converts but many advisory members who shared their dreams, fears, and frustrations of the early days of the program. But, it was not simply a celebration of things past but a reassessment of where we had been, where we were then, and where we were going. Estus reminded the council that it "should never be afraid to accept challenges. If Mississippi moves forward, we must take chances." It was an occasion in which participants from across the state attempted to determine what the council could do to best serve the humanities in Mississippi, asked what had value and meaning, and looked to the future in terms of what we should do and how we could best do it. Several of the conference speakers addressed such questions.

Gary Messinger

Dr. Gary Messinger, our longest serving liaison with the National Endowment for the Humanities, opened the conference with the statement, "If you think times are tough now, you should think back to those early days." He referred to our own Porter Fortune when he addressed the 1973 national meeting and reported that the MHC funded many projects for the "large group of our population . . . that had not gone to high school. . . . These people were as interested as anyone else in this program, and this had been one of the benefits to come from it."

Messenger introduced David Donald, a Pulitzer Prize-winning historian, who reminded us that:

> The Supreme Court of the United States desperately needs an historical staff. In virtually all Supreme Court cases, the research, frankly, is done by elementary law school clerks who have never had

a history seminar, who have no historical training whatsoever. The historical background of some cases is incredibly shoddy.

Estus Smith, our chair at the time, introduced Betsy McCreight from West Virginia, who moderated one of the panels. She told us when West Virginia formed their humanities council, they invited Estus to tell them how to put on a real program! She congratulated the MHC on being one of the five councils in the nation to receive the National Endowment Chairman's Award for Excellence and introduced our two panelists, Dr. Allen Smith and Dr. Otis Graham

Dr. Allen Smith, chairman of the Board for the Law and Humanities Institute and professor of law at Rutgers University [who later joined the faculty of the Mississippi College School of Law], challenged the humanists to play a vital role in the decision-making processes that would shape the future. He cited our Mississippi writers who attracted national and international readers and credited our writers of Mississippi culture for giving an impetus to a worldwide movement toward the humanities. Smith further stated, "A humanist outlook is, today, less of an adornment to life than it is an essential ingredient for survival."

Dr. Otis Graham, distinguished professor of history at the University of North Carolina at Chapel Hill, said:

> The humanities, once thought of as "the classical studies" which probed and borrowed from patterns in Greek and Roman civilizations, are now assumed to be a cluster of disciplines offering approaches to the understanding of Man which are different from the social sciences.

Sarah Rouse

The following morning, Porter Fortune presided at the breakfast honoring the charter members of the MHC. The three selected to talk of the challenges of the early years were Dr. Matthew Page, physician; Dr. Sarah Rouse, dean of humanities at Mississippi College; and Mr. George Howell, vice president and legal counsel of the Marine Group of Litton Industries in Pascagoula.

Dr. Page credited those who put the program together as having done a "masterful job" and found the program the night before "most stimulating." Sarah Rouse, a long-time friend through AAUW, gave me a lot of credit for the accomplishments of the council. I was pleased when Porter Fortune added, "I salute Cora Norman along with the rest of you. Without her assistance and imagination and talent, we never would have gotten where we are."

George Howell

George Howell addressed some of the real problems the council faced in the early days. I quoted most of George's presentation because he described what the members of the council faced in 1972 and how they examined their prejudices. His assessment of the program at that time:

> We found, as we worked through the early years on the council, that our academicians could get down out of the ivory towers into the dusty streets of Mississippi with the non-academicians. During the first years we were organizing, we were establishing our guidelines and feeling our way, and they were challenging times. Once the word got around and people understood the work we were doing and that anyone had access to the help and funding of the council, there was an excess of applications from all types of groups on all types of issues. This was in the early 70s, and we were just coming out of the turbulent 60s and Vietnam. . . . The council meetings were stimulating. At times, the discussions were rather heated as we wrestled with our own views on those issues in deciding the merits of particular programs. You know, learning to accept the notion of granting funds for a program to those with whom you may not agree is a technique in itself. What we were trying to do was to fund discussions in the search for the truth. That, itself, was a novel idea for some of us, who were certain that we already knew all the right answers. . . . The point was that prejudice is taught and learned. We frequently didn't recognize our own prejudices.

> I suppose I feel that one of the great benefits each of us on the council received—I know this is one of the greatest benefits I received—from working together and discussing the issues with people from all shades of background in our state was that

experience of shedding, or more accurately, reducing and refining our own prejudices. Prejudices about white people and black people. Prejudices about academicians. Prejudices about businessmen, about environmentalists, about conservatives, about male chauvinists—and about female chauvinists, Cora. We found that we were all humanistic chauvinists.

As we worked together, discussing together, our knowledge of each other deepened. We learned from each other. We began to understand each other. We became friends working together on the problems of the people of Mississippi. And I shall value these friendships for the rest of my life.

It seems to me that in the numerous confrontations in Mississippi, in the United States, and in the world, and in attempts to resolve these conflicts, the element most lacking is a rational exchange of ideas and views on the real issues. From civilized discussion comes understanding, and from understanding comes peace. . . .Academic humanists and practicing humanists must get more involved. Let me be specific. The real contribution the Mississippi Humanities Council made in the early years to the solution of the problems in Mississippi was to provide funds for people to talk about these problems under the guidelines which injected humanistic ideas and ideals into the discourse. We required that the programs deal with issues of public concern at the grass roots. The issues were controversial. There was controversy on the council. It was hard to administer, and it was controversial in our community and in our state. There were frequent occasions in which we had to write our congressmen and senators explaining what we were about because they were feeling some heat. We funded programs for groups of all sizes on such subjects as racism, the elderly, the environment, emerging feminism, abortion, euthanasia, the poor, the uneducated and many, many more. I am convinced that the discussion of our problems in a humanistic context over the state for the past ten years has enriched public thought in Mississippi and will contribute immeasurable to the improvement of our society. This is a practical application of the humanities, and as a lay humanist I say we need more of it—sponsored by humanists, promoted by humanists, and led by humanists.

I hesitate to make this remark, but from my review of the current list of sponsored programs, it appears that the MHC has drifted from dealing with public policy issues. I would urge you to take a look at the proposals as they come across your desk and return to the principles which we had started in the first five years, and I would urge Gary to reconsider making this a most stringent requirement at the national level.

Let me say a final word about our humanities program here in our state. I believe we can do things in Mississippi to further understanding between people of different views that cannot be done as easily elsewhere. This is the blessing of being in the relatively unsophisticated society of Mississippi. Mississippi holds the promise for finding solutions to many of society's problems if we who believe in the humanities will continue to work for increased presence of the humanities in education and our

public affairs. At present, the most effective vehicle in
Mississippi is this council. . . .We are only beginning
to see the results. A shining example, not specifically
of the work of the council, but influenced greatly by
the work of the council, has been the emergence of
the society of Jackson, Mississippi, from "The Dark
Ages" in the last decade. . . . The work of this council
has been and will continue to be some of the most
important work done in our state for the common
good of the people of Mississippi and people
everywhere. . . . The members of this council have
an exciting challenge and an awesome responsibility.

And so I would conclude my remarks with a charge
to the present members of the Mississippi council.
Do not take your work lightly. Mississippi is a
special place. As we heard last night, Mississippi
has an inordinate influence in the world of literature.
Perhaps Mississippi is destined to play a major role
in the movement which we are about, the infusion of
the humanities into the solution of the problems of
our time. . . .You can have a powerful influence for
change for the common good of mankind.

George Howell was the first council member to serve his
tenure and then later be reappointed to the council.

Dr. Kent Wyatt, president of Delta State University,
introduced our morning lecturer Dr. Peggy Prenshaw. She
was very much involved in the state-based humanities
program from its beginning and always willing to go any
place in Mississippi to be a voice for the humanities. Her
topic for the Tenth Anniversary Conference was "Why the
Humanities in Mississippi?"

Kent Wyatt

Dr. Prenshaw addressed
the practical humanities,
the bread and butter nature
of the humanities. She
chose to give us a model
of a humanist who applied
the humanities in a useful,
down to earth way. She
chose Miss Julia Mortimer,
a fictional school teacher in
a rural Mississippi school
of the 1930s who came
to life in Eudora Welty's
novel *Losing Battles.* She pointed out how Miss Mortimer
took the setting in Mississippi and worked to make school
children aware of their surroundings, to make them look to
the future, and to make them use their minds to make that
future a better place for all people. Dr. Prenshaw ended
her remarks with numerous questions she hoped would be
addressed in the workshops which followed her presentation.

Peggy Prenshaw

There were three concurrent workshops after Prenshaw's
lecture: (1) "Why the Humanities in the Schools?" with Jo

Hollman, moderator; panelists Harriet DeCell Kuykendall, Roy Hudson, Robert E. Wolverton; and Parham H. Williams, Jr., summarizer (2) "Why the humanities in Work?" with Thomasina Blissard, moderator; panelists Stuart Irby, Lynn Crosby Gammill, Peyton W. Williams, Jr.; and Charles Sewell, summarizer (3) "Why the Humanities in Life?" with Joan Cunningham, moderator; panelists Norman Graham, Jason Nichols, June Stevens; and Jerry Ward, summarizer.

Left to right: Harriet DeCell Kuykendall, Roy Hudson, and Robert Wolverton.

Left to right: Thomasina Blissard, Peyton Williams, Stewart Irby, and Lynn Gammill.

Parham Williams and Jo Hollman

After the workshops, conference participants reassembled in the House Chamber of the Old Capitol, where Dr. Estus Smith presented Governor William Winter the Ten Year Report. The Governor accepted the report with compliments to the council for its service to the state and cited the number of programs funded and the range of topics discussed—some controversial. He stated that the public humanities program was possibly the most important and lasting activity in which Mississippians engaged during the past decade. As he was involved in the program prior to becoming governor, he was aware that the programs brought people together across racial lines and that without the public humanities programs those people might not be communicating with each other. He also thanked the members of the council for their commitment to promoting public programs which rationally discussed issues affecting all Mississippians with the inclusion of historical, philosophical and literary aspects. Governor Winter, himself long interested in Mississippi history, noted that such programs were unheard of prior to the formation of the Mississippi Humanities Council.

Following the Governor's remarks, participants congregated on the grounds in front of the War Memorial Building for a buffet luncheon. During my many years in Jackson, it was the only time I saw a group enjoying an outdoor lunch there.

10th Anniversary Picnic

Left to right: George Howell, Parham Williams, and Governor William Winter.

Cora Norman and Porter Fortune

The conference was a memorable experience, as many who participated worked to offer humanities programs in their own communities. I was delighted that my friend David Boileau, executive director of the Louisiana humanities program, came to Mississippi and helped us commemorate our ten years of hard work.

I relied on David's counsel many, many times and traveled with him to work on humanities programs with organized labor and to a weekend retreat at the Rockefeller estate in Arkansas to plan programs for our rural areas. For the first few years, we worked hard to spend the money we received from the NEH, but eventually we started fund-raising. David was the first executive director in the South who raised a significant sum of money for his program. We found that NEH required additional paper work when we accepted outside money, and he lacked that paper work. When confronted by NEH, he said, "You take the donor's money and get the hell out of their way!"

Cora Norman and David Boileau

The date when the Southern Regional Humanities Councils began to form escaped me, but David Boileau was influential in getting the executive directors of the southern states together. He hosted some of our first meetings in New Orleans; we discussed our many challenges and our few successes until the early morning hours at some bar. On one occasion we closed Pat O'Brien's. We never had an agenda, but what a time to rededicate our commitment to the work we were doing! When Robert Cheatham, executive director from Tennessee, came into our midst, he demanded that we set an agenda. "We can't take federal money for travel expenses and not have an agenda for our meetings." After that our meetings never furnished us with the exalting times we enjoyed earlier.

Mississippi hosted two meetings of the Southern Regional Humanities Councils—one on the Gulf Coast and one in Jackson. Following a regional meeting in 1984, Charles Daugherty from West Virginia summed up what we should do at our meetings: focus on one topic, bring in a few outside people to spark our thinking, include board members as well as staff, and host elegant receptions with free time in the evening.

The humanities may not solve all of the mounting practical problems that confront us daily in our modern existence, but they are a key element in the development of mature and educated persons. They deal with the most profound parts of woman's and man's existence—their relationship with the physical world as well as their relationship with the past. The humanities are a measure of the values and aspirations of society, and they reveal the quality of our common life.

In the early 1980s, we worked to get newspapers to publish articles written by humanities professors. Anna Quinn, a teacher in the Booneville Public School System and later at Blue Mountain College, pleaded for the MHC to adopt a program from New Mexico—scholars writing newspapers articles on topics that the humanities might address. In a single day, Anna appeared on a 6 a.m. television program in Tupelo, drove back to Booneville to teach her classes, drove to Greenville for an MHC evening program, and later sang songs with the staff until after midnight.

Charles Dunagin, a newspaper man in McComb, gave us much support as we worked to publicize our programs. He contacted the Mississippi Press Association and asked them to sponsor a project for scholars to write on issues. He suggested the council hold publicity workshops for project directors and involve public relations experts to attract larger audiences and provide greater exposure. He also recommended the formation of a Speaker's Bureau, made up of current and advisory council members, which would provide outlines of available, prepared speeches to interested business and civic groups. Dunagin encouraged the council members to contact their local media to request greater coverage of MHC activities and the staff members to submit more news releases concerning regrants.

We spent much time with proposal writers' workshops. Anna Quinn hosted one such workshop in New Albany, and afterward, the proposal writers admitted how much they learned from the participating scholars. Many of the scholars remarked how much they learned by visiting in the community and talking with citizens.

Although John Guice, professor of history at University of Southern Mississippi, came onto the council in 1980, he was involved almost from the very beginning. Years before I actually met John, I had a long telephone conversation with him when he called to complain about the small $50 honorarium paid to the participating professors in the program. Honoraria were eventually increased. As a member of the council, he reminded the members that evaluations were to be used to improve the MHC funded programs.

Universities cooperated in hosting council activities from the start but gave no recognition to the professors involved. In 1977, I received a letter from a project director concerning the humanist involved in his regrant program—George Mitchell from Jackson State University. "Mr. Mitchell's performance was one of the best I have witnessed. He is particularly talented in captivating the audience, black and white." That particular project director definitely had a frame of reference for his evaluation as he directed several regrants and participated in other programs. I felt it was time for universities to acknowledge professors willing to meet with community groups and immediately wrote to Estus Smith, then vice president of Jackson State University, hoping his university would give that acknowledgment. I hope the institutions of higher learning now give recognition for their professors willing to participate in community programs. After I retired, George Mitchell became a member of the Mississippi Humanities Council.

At a scholar's workshop in Olive Branch in 1981, Dr. Samuel Proctor from Rutgers University addressed the group and reinforced what we tried to do with council funded programs. We wanted the lay citizen who never finished high school to have some idea of the impact of the humanities. Dr. Proctor stated the following:

> The assumption is that the University is the custodian, the trustee of the ideas, the values, the history, and the traditions that give meaning and direction to the society. We have been the legatees of a great trust, and one of the serious challenges that you have been talking about here is that of finding a way to share these ideas and insights with
> a larger society.

For council meetings, I always reserved a suite and usually served drinks the evening prior to the business meeting. Santo Borganelli accompanied his wife Imogene to a council meeting on only one, quite memorable, occasion. We had a real womanizer on the council, and at a very late hour, Imogene and I left the sitting room and retired. Santo decided that he would out-stay the womanizer to ensure that the man left my suite. He thought Imogene went to their hotel room, but she joined me in the bedroom for my protection. Santo served drinks to the unnamed man until he finally saw him out in the wee hours of the morning. When Santo finally got to his room, he found that Imogene was not there. Our unnamed friend was unable to attend the meeting the next morning. He drove to Jackson with another member from his community, but when it was time to leave, he crawled into the back seat of the car and let her drive. Half way home, he insisted that he needed a doctor. She said, knowing nothing about the previous evening, "Oh, you've

Imogene and Santo Borganelli

just had too much to drink." But she stopped at a local hospital. The Borganellis and I never divulged the details of that evening, but I decided to include the story as the unnamed man is now dead.

Imogene and I had many, many trips together, including a humorous one to visit the Neshoba County Fair. They scheduled a midnight "singing," and we went in time for supper with Courtney Tannehill, always our host when we visited the fair. After supper, numerous members of the cabin community invited us in for drinks; we went from cabin to cabin, and it was well after midnight when the singing got underway. By that time, we felt the effects of all those drinks. We left the campground around four or five o'clock in the morning and started our drive back to Jackson. At Carthage I said, "Imogene, I cannot drive another mile." Imogene got behind the wheel, and as soon as we arrived in Jackson, we fell into bed.

Estus Smith's tenure as chair ended in 1982, but he remained on the council until 1984. Afterward, he remained involved with the Federation of State Humanities Councils and their programs and presented a session at their 1991 annual meeting in Providence, Rhode Island. Later, T. W. Lewis reported, "The session presented by Estus Smith of the Kettering Foundation on 'National Issues Forums' was a model for programs dealing with public policy issues."

The resolution presented to Estus when he left the council in 1984 stated, "The MHC, as well as the NEH, will ever bear an Estus Smith mark. We are well aware that many controversial situations but for YOU would have degenerated into acrimony and chaos."

Estus retired as vice president of the Kettering Foundation and returned to Mississippi in 2006. We were saddened that Dorothy died before his return. Friends gathered for a dinner in early 2007 and welcomed him home. Deborah Witte represented the Kettering Foundation that evening, and several claimed the microphone to welcome Estus. I was one of the speakers.

During Estus Smith's tenure as chair, all of the charter members left the council as their tenures expired. One such member was Owen Cooper, who most viewed as a man who had everything—name, recognition, top-notch job, devout Christian faith, and friends everywhere. He once hosted Jimmy Carter in his home in the small town of Yazoo City while Carter campaigned for the presidency. Yet, as Owen looked back on his life, he saw that he could have done more for those who had much less. He left us with the following poem:

IF I HAD MY LIFE TO LIVE OVER

If I had my life to live over,
    I would love more.
I would especially love others more.
I would let this love express itself
    in a concern for my neighbors,
      my friends, and all with whom I came in contact
I would try to let love permeate me,
    overcome me, overwhelm me, and direct me.
I would love the unlovely, the unwanted,
    the unknown, and the unloved.
I would give more. I would learn early in life
    the joy of giving, the pleasure of sharing,
    and the happiness of helping.
I would learn to give more than money.
I would give some of life's treasured possessions,
    such as time, thoughts, and kind words.
If I had my life to live over,
    I would be much more unconventional.
Where society overlooks people,
    I would socialize with them.
Where custom acknowledges peers as best
    with whom to have fellowship,
    I would want some non-peer friends.
Where tradition stratifies people because of
    economics, education, race, or religion,
    I would want to fellowship with friends in all strata.
I would choose to go
    where the crowd doesn't go,
Where the road is not paved,
    where the weather is bitter,
Where friends are few,
    where the need is great,
And where God is most likely to be found.

                      —Owen Cooper

CHARLES SEWELL, CHAIR: 1982-1985

During the first ten years of the council's existence we had only two chairpersons—Porter Fortune and Estus Smith. Each was well known and respected throughout the state and served five years. Their involvement gave the new council recognition that it would not have had with lesser known chairs. The council elected all officers, including chairs, annually. Charter members served their initial term of four years and then drew lots to determine if they would serve an additional one to two years. All subsequent council members served four year terms with reelection sanctioned. In the late 1970s, the council formed an Advisory Council of those who completed their term; membership was a life-time commitment.

Left to right: James Wade, President of Piney Woods School; Peggy Prenshaw; and Charles Sewell.

The Mississippi Humanities Council elected Charles Sewell, an officer with the Deposit Guaranty Bank in Jackson, chair at a meeting at William Carey College on the Gulf Coast in December 1982. Although widely known only in the Jackson area in Mississippi, Charles attended the federation and national meetings as chair and gave us recognition in those groups. He attended a workshop held by the Federation of State Humanities Councils in Salt Lake City, Utah, in 1983 with me and Bill Haynie. At the federation meeting in Atlanta in 1984, the MHC nominated Sewell to the executive board, but he lost to Nancy Stevenson from Illinois. It was difficult in a national election at that time to take on a Stevenson with connections to Adlai Stevenson. Sewell was our official host for the reception the council gave for Bill Bennett when he visited from NEH.

Charles was committed to education and at a council meeting in 1983, after serving as chair for one year, said, "Our audience is the world at large, and we should bring academic excellence to help improve the condition of man." He chaired the Long Range Planning Meeting the council held at the University of Southern Mississippi campus in Long Beach in August 1985. In evaluating MHC's past activities, he commented:

> The next few years are going to be tough ones economically in this state. However, on the political scene, we do have some bright young men [no women?] becoming involved. We must not let the legislature dilute the Education Reform Act as it reevaluates the role of state government.

That was the first time the council took a serious look at its mission, its accomplishments, its failures, and its challenges.

Steve Weiland, from the Federation of State Humanities Councils, was our consultant at that meeting. After listening to some of the stories of our early days, Steve remarked, "This program is so much easier to mount in Minnesota [his home state] than in Mississippi." Ted Alexander went through the planning process to determine: (a) statement of purpose, (b) assessment of prior activities, (c) consistent goals, (d) needed resources, (e) procedures for evaluation, and (f) mechanisms for updating the long-range plan. That retreat provided a refreshing opportunity for MHC members to sit back and together think about the long-term role of MHC in the state.

Leslie Johnson was not one to say very much during council meetings, but he did a good job of summing up what we accomplished as well as future challenges:

> Soul searching has led to adoption of such themes as "Education: The New Horizons," "The Emerging Dream," "Citizens Responsibility to His/Her Institutions: Home, Church, Work, Government," and "The American Centennial Forum." The MHC needs to determine its mission first. If we want proposals from civic and community organizations, how can they be evaluated competitively with those from institutions of higher learning? How can distinguished scholars be recognized? What rewards do scholars receive?

He considered the committee ". . . the single most effective medium which Governor Winter had to bring about the Education Reform Bill" and cited Porter Fortune's words from the Tenth Anniversary Conference: "This program is not for humanists talking to humanists." Les further stated that the tenure of MHC staff and chairpersons was an asset to the program.

As I looked back, I felt we should have looked at proposals from civic organizations differently than those from institutions of higher learning because of the tremendous differences between the targeted audiences. But, our published criteria did not differentiate. During those years, I felt that if we had qualified professors from the humanities, we definitely had a humanities program. Perhaps that was the reason I recommended many of the same professors over and over again.

Charles's wife died suddenly during his tenure, and it was a difficult time for him. After months of sadness, I thought he needed some female companionship. I tried to acquaint him with one of my friends but to no avail. Then, before I realized he was ready to marry again, he told me that he was engaged. We were about to have a meeting of the council in Jackson. I called Frank Riley, a lawyer in Tupelo, and requested he compose a toast; I took bottles of champagne. Frank worked on his toast all the way down the Natchez Trace from Tupelo. Charles came without his fiancée and made some excuse that she played tennis that day and hurt her back. Days later we found that the marital arrangement was canceled. I gave up trying to be a matchmaker.

Frank Riley was much involved in the council's meetings. Always available to give us legal advice, he prepared our incorporation papers and, in 1983, announced that the MHC was officially incorporated. One of the council's more memorable evenings was a dinner hosted by Frank and his wife in their home in Tupelo. Jack Reed, a Tupelo businessman and well-known Mississippian, met with us that night. He was a leading politician in the state and ran unsuccessfully for governor.

I was indebted to many of the council members for their support and involvement in public humanities programs. Dollye Robinson, a long-time professor of music at Jackson State University, was involved from the beginning. Once, when I called a press conference, not one person from the media was there at the appointed hour. Dollye went to the telephone, and in a very few minutes, we had three press members at our meeting. She saved my day. Today (2009), she serves as dean of the School of Liberal Arts at JSU.

Jerry Ward, Jr. was a popular scholar with groups planning public humanities programs. He taught at Tougaloo College but took a leave of absence in 1985 to spend a year at the National Endowment for the Humanities. At a council meeting in 1984, Jerry gave the following assessment of our program:

Jerry Ward, Jr.

During the twelve years the MHC has funded programs, I have observed significant changes in the intellectual life of the state. Prior to the 1970s, the intellectuals among us had little direct contact with large numbers of Mississippians; they pursued the life of the mind in isolation. MHC programs have enabled scholars in the humanities to maintain a continuing dialogue with people who might have thought learning ended on the night of high school graduation. To be sure, the real impact of MHC programs is difficult to measure. We don't have a head count on the number of people who have begun reading more or asking more enlightened questions as a result of the new dialogue. The impact is virtually non-quantitative, and it should be. For the intellectual life of a state is not to be sought in graphs and statistics. It is found in the conversations that citizens have about matters of immediate and long-range concern and in their willingness to interrelate the accumulated knowledge of the past with the emerging problems of the present and future. That process the MHC has accelerated.

In 1997, he received the council's Humanities Scholar Award. Jerry is now at Dillard University in New Orleans.

In 1983 before Gary Messinger left the NEH, the MHC prepared a resolution and gave it to Bill Bennett for presentation to Gary. In preparing it I found only three brief notes in our files, even though Gary was our liaison for six or seven years. He usually observed our meetings silently and then gave his true evaluation when he returned to Washington, D. C. However, on two occasions he came and stayed longer than I expected. What was I to do with him after the council meetings? The Mississippi State Fair was in full swing in Jackson on one of those occasions, so I decided that we would take in the fair. The next time Gary planned to stay in Jackson overnight, I drove him to Philadelphia to the Neshoba County Fair. We had lunch with Courtney Tannehill, who had a cabin very near Founders Square, and then watched the sulky races. He probably saw Mississippi in a new light after that visit. I was certainly honored when Gary later wrote and asked that I write a letter of recommendation for him as he was leaving the NEH. He was a man of few words but always there when we called.

The MHC hosted a meeting of the Southern Regional Humanities Councils in 1984 on the Mississippi Gulf Coast. Mary Benjamin, Jackson State University, and Joan Cunningham, Meridian Community College, were much involved in that meeting, as were Hazel Portwood and Bill Haynie, who both lived on the coast. Bill and his wife hosted the entire group at a dinner in their home.

As dean of liberal arts at JSU, Mary organized a Community Advisory Council to the School of Liberal Arts, one of the first in the country. To that council, she named Charles Sewell, Dollye Robinson, and myself as members. In 1984, I also represented the MHC in the academic procession at the inauguration of the new president at JSU, Dr. James Hefner. It was the first time the MHC received recognition as an educational agency in such an activity.

Joan Cunningham hosted meetings as well as programs at Meridian Community College. In referring to regrant programs, she stated, "Our position is analogous to that of Sisyphus; except in our case, the rock which we are pushing up the hill not only rolls back down before we reach the top but also increases in size with each pushing." From 1978, when Bill Scaggs came onto the council, throughout the remainder of my tenure, we had members from Meridian as well as additional leadership from Evelyn Polk, Allye Fae Turner, and Gregory Lane. MHC programs were well publicized by the media in that area.

It seemed that the council never ceased discussing its mission or how they were succeeding in accomplishing it. At least once a year, and especially while orienting new council members, the mission and the type of programs funded were always topics on the agenda. At one such meeting, William T. McGehee from Cleveland stated, "Let's get over this passive waiting for requests for programs; the MHC should be aggressive."

During the mid-to-late 1980s, I was also involved with AAUW's activities and a member of their national board. I ran for president of the AAUW Foundation at the meeting in San Francisco. Although Imogene Borganelli was on crutches at the time, she insisted on going to that meeting with me. Bobbie Oatis, dean of women at Jackson State University, said to me prior to the trip, "You've got to have some help with your enunciation of AAUW; Malena Dow is going to tutor you." And Malena, who taught speech at JSU, did. When we got to San Francisco, I found I had two minutes at the microphone to give my reasons for running. Imogene helped me rehearse by timing me. She found that I used a full minute to say *A-A-U-W*. Finally, Imogene said, "Eliminate the name—just don't use it!" I lost the election.

Imogene Borganelli and Cora Norman

On our way home, Bobbie informed me that one of those elected was also from Arkansas and "pronounced *A-A-U-W* just as you do, Cora." It doesn't pay to try to change your background!

Peggy Prenshaw, Chair: 1985-1987

Peggy Prenshaw

Peggy Prenshaw was involved in the program from its beginning. She attended the meeting held at University of Southern Mississippi during the planning stage and from that day on was an integral part of the state humanities program. In the early days, Dr. Melerson Guy Dunham from Prentiss had many MHC programs and always had Peggy and Leslie Burl McLemore as her scholars. Dr. Dunham held one of her more memorable programs in Columbia, memorable because she followed it with a political meeting. She announced at the conclusion of the MHC program that she also set up a meeting with Democratic leaders from Jackson, including Claude Ramsey, head of the AFL-CIO in Mississippi. In order to end the humanities meeting, she asked that everyone go outside and then return if they wished to attend the political meeting. Peggy and I, both being Democrats, decided immediately; we exited the humanities program and returned for the political meeting!

In those early days of the program, professors received the "large" honorarium of $50. Invited to Philadelphia, Mississippi, for an entire day, Peggy met with a group at the library for a brown bag luncheon and then spent the afternoon with students at the high school. Philadelphia is miles away from Hattiesburg, but she received the usual $50. The meager honorarium attracted few professors, and John Guice telephoned me long before I ever met him to complain about it. It was several years before honorariums increased.

In 1985, Peggy allowed me to accompany a group from University of Southern Mississippi to England, where she taught the course "Contemporary British Women Writers" at the University of London. It was a wonderful experience to attend her lectures each morning, take off for some

Left to right: Peggy Prenshaw, Modena Martin, and Cora Norman

recommended pub for lunch, attend a program at night, and then return to the dormitory for a discussion of the day's activities. While there, we made a weekend trip to Scotland. Maureen Ryan, another professor from USM, drove us and left London at 80 MPH! We stayed at the University Club in Edinburgh, and while registering, a man, who sat silently as we entered, spoke up and asked about our president at USM, Aubrey Lucas. He met Aubrey in California; it is a small world.

Following Jane Hiatt's departure, the council selected Dr. Barbara Carpenter, who had a background in literature, as assistant director. Later, she edited *Ethnic Heritage in Mississippi*. Journalist Norma Fields wrote at the time that the book should be required reading for every citizen, or at least every citizen who had not already studied the cultural variety in our state. Following Hurricane Katrina, which devastated the Mississippi Gulf Coast, Barbara brought national recognition to the council for her work with community organizations in that part of the state.

Left to right: Celia Booth, Cora Norman, and Brenda Gray

Celia Booth joined us as secretary in 1986 and remained in that position until after I retired. Her demeanor—always smiling—added much to the ambience of our office. She also received her associate of art's degree from Hinds Community College in 1991 while helping us with the humanities program. I appreciated the support she gave me in her position.

By 1986, the council received publicity from two sources other than its regrant programs. Governor Allain appointed me to serve on the commission to plan commemorative activities in Mississippi in celebration of Martin Luther King's birthday. And the Ole Miss alumni magazine did a three page feature article on the MHC and its support of an incredibly broad array of programs in communities in every part of the state. An excerpt from that article:

> . . . Professors and townsfolk have exchanged ideas on rural traditions and new technologies, on Choctaw culture and Southern fiction, Biblical roots and the realities of arms control, the role of small hospitals, the merits of a new school building, family tensions, nuclear waste, the coastal environment, the folk music of the hills, the defense budget, and the changing roles of women, blacks, school teachers, and newspapers have all received discussion in meetings held throughout the state. . . .

The article quoted Tom Flynn and referred to his beliefs that the general public viewed professors as somewhat isolated with little rapport with those who lived in rural communities and that many in the general public had never seen a professor, much less met one. It stated that the rural citizens liked talking, and even arguing, with the professors and that "those who receive the most credit for the committee's success are Dr. Fortune, Dr. Smith, and Dr. Cora Norman, executive director."

Celia Emmerich, a daughter-in-law of our charter member J. O. Emmerich, promoted programs in the Greenville area. In 1986, she hosted a public meeting in Congressional District II in order that the public could have input into MHC plans. That meeting attracted a new audience, and its program devoted time to distinguishing the arts and the humanities.

In 1986, the Federation of State Humanities Councils decided their headquarters needed to be in Washington, D. C. Steve Weiland resigned, and Jamil Zainaldin became head of the organization. In September, the federation elected Peggy Prenshaw to its board. President Aubrey Lucas of USM later hosted a dinner for council members at his home in order to honor her; she was dean of the Honors College at USM at that time.

In 1987, Peggy testified on behalf of the federation before the Congressional Subcommittee on the Interior. While

Peggy Prenshaw and Cora Norman

Peggy, Ed Bishop, and I were in Washington at the federation meeting, our own Representative Jamie Whitten attended his first humanities program. He headed the Appropriations Committee in the House of Representatives, and we kept Jamie apprised of our activities from the very beginning. Our files contained several letters from him. At the breakfast meeting, Jamie told others that Prenshaw and Norman had "educated" him.

As Peggy's year on the federation board was about to expire, there were no nominations for the position of president. Jamil Zainaldin, executive director of the federation, called me to discuss Peggy's nomination for the position. I was dubious but felt with more time on the board Peggy would be a shoe in. However, the Mississippi council nominated her. Just before the deadline for nominations, our former adversary Nancy Stevenson announced that she was running, and we again lost to her! For some time, I thought Jamil should not have intervened, and my relationship with him remained cool for some time. Later, I realized that he recognized that Peggy Prenshaw had what he needed—the ability to talk to legislators! When I retired, I received some very nice notes, but Jamil's note was the one I treasured most.

Peggy continued to be a recognized leader on the federation board and in 1988 was instrumental in developing a literacy conference held at Ohio State University, jointly sponsored by the Federation of State Humanities Councils and the Modern Language Association. Barbara Carpenter, now executive director of the MHC, participated in that conference.

Several members of the Mississippi Humanities Council have served on the board of the federation—Estus Smith first; then Peggy Prenshaw, Leslie Burl McLemore, and Willis Lott, who is now (2009) chair of the federation. I was pleased to learn that the entire federation board supported Willis for chair.

Thanks to Porter Fortune and George Howell, we learned very early in Mississippi to keep our congressional delegation apprised of our activities. When in Washington, members of our council and I always visited offices of the Mississippi delegation, and we always mailed our printed materials to their Washington offices. While B. J. Stiles was at the NEH, he and I visited Jamie Whitten. B. J. wanted to talk about the NEH appropriation. We got in to see Whitten, who entertained us for thirty minutes about his early experiences teaching school in a one-room school house in Mississippi. He was in no hurry to get us out of his office. After we left, B. J. expressed his disappointment in not addressing NEH's needs. I said to him, "When Representative Whitten gives us thirty minutes of his time, you can count on his help in the Appropriations Committee."

At a federation breakfast in Washington in 1988, we had not only Representative Jamie Whitten with us, but Representatives Espy and Dowdy and an aide from Senator Stennis' office, all from Mississippi. Other members of the federation certainly noted Jamie Whitten's presence. A congressman from one of the other states commented, "You don't need me; you have Jamie Whitten!" Other Mississippians who attended that breakfast with Whitten were Ted Alexander, president of Pearl River Community College; Peggy Prenshaw; Ed Bishop, Mayor of Corinth; Barbara Carpenter, and myself.

In 1987, in preparing a statement of commendation for Peggy's service as chair of the MHC, Jerry Ward wrote:

> You have been our Julia Mortimer, never doubting ". . . but that all worth preserving is going to be preserved, and all we had to do was keep it going, right from where we are, one teacher on down to the next." . . . Your insistence that we truly understand the sense of place in our heritage, our work on the Mississippi Mindscape project, your election to the Executive Board of the Federation of State Humanities Councils, the benefit of your wisdom as we revised the 1985 MHC Long-Range Plan, your ideas for new directions that persuaded us to change our name to the Mississippi Humanities Council, my feeling exceptionally proud when you were hailed as a champion on the front page of *Humanities Discourse*, for your stunning testimony before the United States House of Representatives' Appropriations Subcommittee on the Interior on behalf of the NEH and the state councils. The largest nuggets of gold embodied our knowledge that you are a scholar and humanist with a purpose, one who believes literature "gives pleasure, educates the imagination, and engenders compassion and tolerance, even detachment as it motivates people to action." They contain also your perspicacity about the twin dangers of aliteracy and illiteracy, your determining that our council's "most basic function is to encourage and help empower a full literacy" among the citizens of Mississippi. That definition speaks volumes about your genuine respect and love for people.

Peggy Prenshaw's service to the federation attracted national attention, and in 1994, she received a Frankel Prize from the National Endowment for the Humanities. President Clinton later appointed her to the National Advisory Board of the NEH.

At the long-range planning meeting held in 1985, the council adopted a plan which included continuing assessments. So in 1987, the Long-Range Planning Committee, composed of Henry Hobbs, chair; Harriet DeCell; T. W. Lewis, III; Luther Munford; Dollye Robinson; Jerry W. Ward, Jr.; and Peggy Prenshaw, presented the amended long-range plan, "A Society in Transition":

> Our basic function is to encourage and help empower full literacy among all people of the state, a rich and vital literacy that dispels ignorance and powerlessness, that leads to understanding of our history and the civilizations and cultures of others, that gives each of us a realistic opportunity to live in freedom and dignity. That is the charge of the humanities. While Mississippi has made great progress, this is still a state where forty-five percent of our adults have not graduated from high school. Mississippi is a "society in transition," thus a fertile ground for a humanities program, and a place where investment in "promoting the humanities in public life" is likely to yield large returns.

While chair of the council, Peggy appointed a program committee for the fifteenth anniversary program held in December 1987. Members Henry Hobbs, chair; Rosia Crisler; Carey Hearn; and Jerry Ward worked with me and Barbara Carpenter.

Henry Hobbs was very active in the program while on the council. In 1987, he hosted a luncheon at his home for members of the Long-Range Planning Committee. Early in his tenure, he wrote to me suggesting that we do a program on the black dialect. With race relations tense in Mississippi at that time, I thought it was too early for such a topic. However in recent years, the Natchez Literary Conference hosted such a program, indicating how times changed in Mississippi. Comments from the resolution presented to Henry at the time of his retirement from the council included:

> He has . . . by the excellence with which he has practiced his profession of the law, exemplified the values to which the humanities would inspire commitment, and has encouraged public discussion, debate and dialogue without which humane societies do not thrive. . . . An example of vintage Hobbs: In response to our director's appeal that he befriend and cultivate at an upcoming orientation conference the members of the newly established Virgin Islands Humanities Council on the chance that they reciprocate and invite the MHC to the Islands, Henry wrote in reply: "Never had much luck with virgins, and at my age and state of infirmity, it wouldn't make much difference if I did; but for the council's sake, I'll do what I can. . . ."

James Wade, president of Piney Woods School, was an ardent member of the council. His faculty planned a meeting on the Gulf Coast and wanted Duke University's Dr. John Hope Franklin, the nation's most outstanding black historian, to speak. They asked me to call him, and I did. He was most gracious over the telephone and agreed to come. We held the program in Biloxi, but before he left the state, he took a tour of Piney Woods School. Several years later, they wanted Dr. Franklin to return and asked if I would call again. I did, and he agreed to return to Piney Woods. When Dr. Wade retired, Dr. Beady became president, and I gave a testimonial to Dr. Wade. The high points of my speech included:

> . . . It seems that we forget why we are in the business of education—to teach students, to provide an atmosphere where a young person can grow intellectually, develop self-confidence, develop a set of values, be able to articulate his or her ideas, and to mold a vision for living. Dr. Wade never forgot, and he never let those around him forget that Piney Woods exists to help students. . . .

> He is a first-class fund raiser because he had a purpose for the money—students. Now I think what has impressed me most about this rare man has been the way he takes a significant occasion like Founders Day and graduation and gives recognition to deserving students and to their parents. His students have given "Founders Day Statements" that make many of us who are recognized public speakers hang our heads in shame. On one such occasion a young girl had performed admirably at Founders Day and the audience clapped enthusiastically. Dr. Wade called that young woman back to the podium and told us about another accomplishment of hers. She had made the lovely suit she was wearing that day and he asked that she model for the audience. His recognition of her sewing ability made many of us envious that we lacked the ability to do likewise. . . .

In a publication, after you took over from the founder of Piney Woods, Dr. Laurence Jones, you were quoted, "It's not easy to succeed a legend. Dr. Jones left some mighty big shoes to fill, and I am still rattling around in them." Well, Dr. Beady, one might think that you will be stumbling all over the place with one foot rattling around in Dr. Laurence Jones' shoe and the other foot rattling around in Dr. James Wade's shoe except for the fact that Dr. Wade always went looking for the best when he wanted a teacher, a speaker, OR his successor. We wish you well, Dr. Beady.

When James Wade left the presidency at Piney Woods, he moved to Florida, and we maintained a correspondence until his death.

The council was fortunate to claim Luther Munford, an attorney in Jackson, for membership. He was a personal friend of Sheldon Hackney, who became chairman of the National Endowment for the Humanities after Luther completed his tenure on the council. Luther drafted the first long-range plan submitted to the NEH, a document both workable and brief due to its concise language. It received accolades. He brought to the MHC rich personal and professional resources from an academic career that included Princeton and Oxford Universities as well as the University of Virginia School of Law, from experience as a clerk with the United States Supreme Court and earlier with the U. S. Court of Appeals, and from his practice of law. He later returned to academe as an associate professor at the Mississippi College School of Law. As treasurer of the council, Luther signed nothing without proper and complete documentation, thereby assuring that in the dispensing

of public monies all transactions were exemplary. He
was a strong advocate of using the media to disseminate
council and other humanities-related programs. He served
as counsel to the staff in working with Governor Allain in
the heroic, but unsuccessful, effort to have the Mississippi
council designated as the official agency for promoting the
bicentennial of the U. S. Constitution. He was the person
most qualified to keynote the Fifteenth Anniversary of the
council's activities and did so with his splendid address "The
Impact of the New York Times vs. Sullivan on Politics in
Mississippi."

Left to right: Ed Bishop, Luther Munford, and Leslie
McLemore

TED ALEXANDER, CHAIR: 1987-1988

Jane Bryan and Ted Alexander

Ted Alexander, a graduate of Millsaps College, came on the council knowing what the humanities were all about. He was also a member of the Rotary Club in McComb. Council members were not aware that the McComb Rotary Club had a member on the Mississippi Humanities Council for sixteen consecutive years. Oliver Emmerich was a charter member of the council and during his last year nominated Newton James. In his recommendation, he said, "The council needs a storyteller, and Newt is your man." As Newt was about to leave the council, he nominated Charles Dunagin of the McComb newspaper *Enterprise-Journal*, who later brought Ted Alexander to the council membership. There was a lapse before we had another Rotarian on the council—Newton Ward James, Newt's son, who came to the council in 1994.

At the time Ted came to the council, he was superintendent of the McComb Public Schools. He later became president of Pearl River Community College in Poplarville. He probably knew more about the humanities than any president of our community colleges. With Ted's leadership, we began to make some inroads with the community colleges. In 1987, he pointed out to the council that Mississippi—a state in which one half of the population over 16 had no high school diploma—put fewer dollars into literacy programs than any other state.

Judge William C. Keady, United States District Court Northern District of Mississippi, came onto the council while Ted was chair. I met Keady earlier when he chaired the Bicentennial Commission appointed by Governor Allain; I was a member of that commission. We were planning a gala evening for the judiciary, the congressional delegation, and politicians. I thought the evening should be open to anyone who wanted to attend, so I took it upon myself to write a letter to the judge:

> . . . The Constitution touches all Americans. . . . Blacks and women should be visible at the podium. . . . In 1987, we must show that blacks are full-fledged citizens in our state. . . . The women should be represented not by Southern belles to adorn the affair but by women who deal with the text of the constitution daily—teachers, social workers, writers, newspaperwomen, and young women.

I got a reply that a black minister could give the invocation and a woman might sing for the group. However, the occasion never materialized; Judge Keady had problems with Governor Allain and resigned from the Commission.

In December 1988, the *Clarion-Ledger* in Jackson carried an article, "Volunteering Can Create Changes," by Rebecca Hood-Adams:

What law cannot coerce, caring inspires.

On the surface, racism, classism and discrimination against the elderly or handicapped yield to legislation. But real social change—diminishing prejudice—is often effected through volunteerism.

It took three years to find a meeting room where blacks and whites could, and would, sit side-by-side to discuss education in Holmes County.

In 1972, there were few places in the Delta for an integrated public discussion of the humanities. So Cora Norman, executive director of the Mississippi Humanities Council, brought together professors from universities across the state at a small radio station in Lexington.

"We had lines installed for the public to call in," she said. "But in the five months we were on the air, there was not a single telephone call. The people weren't used to interacting. . . .

The next year, Norman held meetings at Lexington Attendance Center, a public school that had been effectively rendered all black after desegregation spurred white flight to private schools. Although the meetings were open to everyone, only blacks attended. . . .

"Volunteerism certainly has an effect on social problems," said Bettye McPhail, coordinator for Jackson's Information Referral Outreach and Senior Security Programs. "When you get involved, you see what life is actually like instead of stereotypes. That's what it takes to build a community."

Norman believes the natural personality of a volunteer fosters understanding.

"These people enter the arena with the idea of interaction with people different from themselves," she said. "They become more tolerant from batting their ideas around and defending them. That doesn't mean they always agree, but they do show respect."

Largely due to Porter Fortune's leadership, we called everyone on the council by their first name, including Porter. Having worked on the campus of the University of Mississippi prior to joining the MHC, I knew that everyone on campus referred to him as Chancellor Fortune and there were no exceptions. So, when Judge Keady came onto the council, I went directly to Ted Alexander and said, "The ambiance of the council will be destroyed if we call Bill Keady, Judge Keady." Ted made his stand with one sentence, "Cora, if you've ever been in Judge Keady's courtroom, you will not call him Bill!" Well, I decided that since I was never in his courtroom, I would call him Bill. I addressed my letters to Bill, and prior to a council meeting I always told myself, "Tomorrow, I shall call him Bill." Although when I saw the man coming toward me the next day, I greeted him face to face as Judge Keady!

While Keady was on the council, Ted hosted a council dinner in the new president's home at Pearl River Community College. I knew that Keady always had his dinner at six in the evening and informed Ted of that. Ted simply replied, "Judge Keady's dinner will be ready at 6 p.m." When we left the president's home that evening to drive back to our lodging in Hattiesburg, Judge Keady got on one bus and his federal marshal bodyguard mistakenly got on another. The marshal's bus got to Hattiesburg first, and that was one upset bodyguard until he saw Keady's bus pull in!

T. W. LEWIS, III, CHAIR: 1988-1991

T. W. Lewis, III

A no-nonsense chair of the Mississippi Humanities Council, T.W. Lewis knew what he stood for, and he stood up for his beliefs. During his tenure as chair, he probably had the most dedicated council members since those who held charter membership. Almost half the council members who served while T. W. was chair were involved with the program from the very beginning—Ben Bailey, Ed Bishop, Jane Bryan, Velvelyn Foster, Sid Graves, Linda Kay, Harriet DeCell Kuykendall, Charles Lowery, Jeanne Luckett, John Peterson, Peggy Prenshaw, and Robert Walker. I took the liberty in the following paragraphs to convey a little of what each contributed.

Ben Bailey of Tougaloo College served on the council from 1988 to 1992. He was one of the earliest scholars involved in the state-based program and was part of the first group of scholars ever convened to write model proposals for me to offer to non-profit groups for MHC funding. Ben also wrote several letters to the editor of *The Clarion-Ledger* and gave the MHC credit for making an impact on our state; one in 1986 stated:

> Mississippi Authority for Education Television and the Mississippi Committee for the Humanities, under the leadership of Cora Norman, have done more for education in Mississippi's out-of-school population than any other entity in the state. I have seen horizons broaden and people's ideas about each other change as a result of the programs of these two agencies.

Ben Bailey

In 1989, Ben presented to the council a long-range plan which was accepted unanimously; the council expressed much appreciation for his work. In 1990, T. W. Lewis announced that NEH approved our planning grant of $10,000 for the Long-

Range Planning Retreat. Jamil Zainaldin was our consultant. The retreat, which focused on leadership, was at Cedar Grove, an antebellum home in Vicksburg. Jamil understood so well what we were about in the state humanities councils, and he articulated our mission in a forthright manner. He stated:

> It is our business to remind people that each is endowed with the "human spirit" which brings hope in a world that often gives little ground for hope; which instills a quest for justice in a world which is not always committed to justice; is capable of loving in a world that is often lonely and unloving; that brings a hunger to understand theory that eludes understanding; a human spirit with the capacity for awe, wonder, imagination and reverence. As a group we must constantly remind ourselves that the human spirit is a spring that never completely dries up.

At dinner, Ben, seated at the head of the table, remarked, "I never thought I would be seated at the head of the table here at Cedar Grove." Race relations were different by that time.

During Ben's stellar academic career as professor and chair of the music department at Tougaloo College, as head of the humanities division, and as director of institutional research, he was also involved with the state-based humanities program as scholar, project director, and promoter of quality public humanities programs. He was always concerned with reaching and educating grassroots groups.

Ed Bishop was another council member who was involved from the start and became a member of the council in 1987. Because of his lengthy contacts with our congressional delegation in Washington—especially Representative

Jamie Whitten and Senator Thad Cochran—I was able to get to them. I not only got time with Representative Bennie Thompson, but Ed saw to it that we had a picture to take back to use for publicity in Mississippi.

Left to right: Ed Bishop,
Representative Bennie Thompson,
and Cora Norman.

Left to right: Ed Bishop, Representative
Jamie Whitten, and Cora Norman.

I served on the national board of the American Association of University Women from 1985 to 1989, and we always stayed at the Watergate Hotel, now closed, when meeting in Washington. I often used the occasion to host a reception at the Watergate Hotel for our congressional delegation and people from the National Endowment for the Humanities. Ed Bishop was there for one such gathering standing in the middle of the room, holding his glass of wine, and entertaining guests all evening.

Ed was always available when called. He spent three days with us at Winrock Farms in Arkansas, where we developed programs that examined rural values and ways in which they had changed or vanished in today's more urban settings. When he became mayor of Corinth, he was instrumental in getting the MHC on the program of the annual Municipal Association Meeting on the Gulf Coast. Ed had no hesitation in approaching any person or foundation, congressional leader or state legislator, to solicit funds for public humanities programs. He went with the MHC's staff to Savannah, Georgia, to attend a fund raising seminar and practically took over the session on the nuts and bolts of fund raising.

Cora Norman and
Ed Bishop

Because of Bishop's influence, the MHC usually claimed more of their congressional delegation than any other state at the annual Humanities on the Hill Breakfast, held to inform the congressional members about public humanities programs. They came because they knew that Ed Bishop was in the audience. Representative Jamie Whitten held the powerful position of chair of the House Appropriations Committee, but members of the Mississippi council were always welcome to visit Jamie's office and to stay as long as they wished because of Ed.

Following one of the federation meetings with congressmen in Washington, Roscoe Boyer of the University of Mississippi sent me a copy of a newspaper picture of Ed, Senator Thad Cochran, and myself. Ed wrote a letter thanking Dr. Boyer and said:

> Interestingly enough, I was one among the first minorities to attend the initial meeting of the Humanities Council, which was held at the University, under the direction of Dr. Norman. That was long before desegregation. Believe it or not, we ate dinner in the Commons. Many of the first humanities programs were funded for communities in northeast Mississippi. Cora is to be congratulated for both her imagination and courage during these many years as Director of the Mississippi Humanities Council. It is one among the best in the country.

It is a long drive from Corinth to Jackson—over 400 miles round trip—but Ed Bishop never hesitated to make that drive when called to a meeting in Jackson. He also never declined because of other duties when I requested that he accompany me to Washington, D. C. In his later years, his knees gave him a lot of pain. When we arrived on the Hill in Washington, we took taxis from one building to another, but once inside the congressional buildings, the halls were extremely long. I knew Ed was in agony. But when I tried to curtail some of the visits, Ed always said, "We've got to do it." Despite his throbbing knees, he stayed with me to make those calls.

In early 1996, I was aware that Ed's health was failing. I visited him while he was in the hospital in Jackson. Shortly after he returned to his home in Corinth, I received the call that he was in the Tupelo hospital, dying. I jumped into my car in Jackson, drove the 159 miles to Tupelo, went into his room, gave him a kiss, and returned to Jackson that evening with a very heavy heart. I lost a very good friend.

Jane Bryan, who served on the council from 1991 to 1996, was one of our earliest project directors. While director of the McComb Library, she received funding for a program that explored the reluctance of local college graduates to return home. As director of the library system in Pascagoula, she continued to provide programs for the council. She arranged a leadership seminar on civic virtue in 1991 and in 1992 sponsored a reception to present "Ethnic Heritage in Mississippi." Jane traveled across the country to represent the MHC at national and regional meetings. At the Southern Regional Humanities Councils meeting in Savannah, Georgia, she helped me host our usual reception for that group. Following the meeting, Ron Benson, executive director of the Georgia program, arranged a tour of Ossabaw Island. Jane and I went on the tour—a memorable event— and returned to our Savannah hotel room dirtier than either of us had ever been.

Left to right: Michael Sartisky, Cora Norman, and Chuck Daugherty.

Bryan urged the MHC forward into the 21st century through her interest in electronic media and programming using the internet, interactive video, and other forward-looking projects. At the 1994 federation meeting in San Antonio, she participated on a panel discussing "New Technologies for the Humanities." Jane and I had several trips together—cruises on the Mississippi River and in the Gulf of Mexico. She was a great travel companion and always ready for a get together!

Left to right: Jane Bryan, Katharine Rea, and Cora Norman.

Dr. Velvelyn Foster, professor at Jackson State University, served four years as a governor's appointee to the MHC from 1988 to 1992. However, this was but a small part of her contributions to the MHC. She participated for many years as project director and scholar for numerous programs working with teachers to enhance their skills in social studies and to improve the humanities in general in public education.

As a member of the council, Velvelyn attended many of our regrant programs. She was our community liaison when we promoted a program in Bogue Chitto, where she was raised. Once, when I visited there with her, she introduced me to her mother, of whom I asked how she endured the days of oppression of blacks in Mississippi. She replied, "I was the best dancer in the county." That said a lot for how we use our leisure time!

Left to right: Sid Graves, Cora Norman, Jamil Zainaldin, and Billy Thames.

Sid Graves, also on the council from 1988 to 1992, hosted many of our programs while director of the Clarksdale Library and served as an outside evaluator for many others. His enormous vitality and endless enthusiasm brought writers, artists, scholars, and musicians alike to rural Mississippi. A near genius for promotion and publicity, he sponsored programs certain of an audience. As president of the Mississippi Library Association, he included the MHC staff and its programs in MLA activities and ensured that the MHC received recognition. Sid died at an early age after moving from Clarksdale to Hattiesburg.

Linda Kay, Mississippi Department of Education, was an energetic and enthusiastic supporter of the council and its activities during her tenure as member from 1989 to 1993 and was faithful in attending meetings and programs. She lent her expertise to the development and implementation of regrants and revived interest in geography education, global education, the U. S. Constitution, and our Bill of Rights.

As a member of the Screening Committee, Linda responded quickly to proposals and devoted careful attention and assessment skills to weighing their merits. She was always available to consult with staff on program possibilities and to pass along such information to a wide network of teachers.

Linda also increased the visibility of the MHC through her activities. She attended a session with Governor Mabus when he received the annual report, the press conference when Lynne Cheney presented "Ethnic Heritage in Mississippi" to the public, and the NEH Orientation Conference in Jacksonville, Florida, She entered into all discussions with vigor—clearly demonstrating the MHC's leadership in regional groups.

Linda Kay discharged her responsibilities as a council member in exemplary fashion with wit, wisdom, and tolerance. I was impressed with the time she gave to MHC activities in addition to the demands of a career, the responsibilities of caring for an invalid mother, a commitment to preserving the environment, and full participation in her church's activities. Women at University of Southern Mississippi organized the Culture Club with Linda's help as they prepared for their outstanding symposium, "Images '79." The group evolved into a women's club, traveling together internationally as well as frequently getting together in Mississippi. They let me join a few years later.

Culture Club

Harriet DeCell Kuykendall was not only a member of the council from 1987 to 1991 but also a long-time project director of many regrants, including the newspaper project. She was involved in the work of the council from its beginning and served on staff during my first sabbatical. She encouraged numerous groups to apply for funding for public projects and called upon prospective donors. Once, after Deposit Guaranty Bank turned her down, she immediately walked across the street to Unifirst Bank while devising her presentation and left with funding. Her first husband Senator Herman DeCell was involved in our early programs as well.

After his death, Harriet married Kuykendall, who greatly supported our endeavors. They entertained groups in their home many times.

Governor Bill Allain appointed Charles D. Lowery, professor of history at Mississippi State University, to the MHC in 1986. He served until 1991 and often represented the chair as the council elected him vice chair three times. He faithfully attended council meetings, often worked with the staff to conduct public meetings, sought funding from donors in his area, and attended many council-funded programs in all parts of the state. Charles often brought the MHC staff and the MSU faculty together, hosted luncheons for groups on his campus, and entertained NEH Program Officer Malcolm Richardson.

Jeanne Luckett served on the council from 1990 to 1994 but was involved with MHC programs from the very early days. As a media consultant, she helped with many of our programs and became chair in 1993.

John Peterson

John Peterson was a member of the council from 1989 to 1992, but he and Peyton Williams planned and conducted the very first meeting the MHC held at Mississippi State University. It was during our organizational period in 1972 when we asked citizens to identify issues facing Mississippi at that time. John was most helpful in involving the Choctaws, who were funded for a program during our first year of regrants. He and Charles Lewis from MSU were leaders at an early Academic Humanists' Workshop in Jackson. John spent time in Zimbabwe and was preparing to return when he found that he had cancer; he died shortly thereafter. The council prepared "In Memoriam" after John's death:

> John Peterson is honored for the moral integrity and intellect he exhibited in the Mississippi Humanities Council over the years; his moral support to other professors who were dubious about participating in a public program on a controversial issue in Olive Branch; the wealth of ideas he offered to the staff; his ability to address an issue directly and put his thoughts into writing to share with the council, and particularly his essay in "Ethnic Heritage in Mississippi" and John Peterson is fondly remembered by the Mississippi Humanities Council for his informative, humorous travelogues from Zimbabwe and the love of people he exuded through these and other actions.

Peggy Prenshaw served as chair of the MHC from 1985 to 1987 and continued her membership on the Council until 1991. She was involved with programs from the inception.

Robert Walker, on the council from 1989 to 1993, truly helped us launch a public humanities program in Mississippi. While a graduate student in history at Ole Miss in the mid-seventies, he worked several hours each week writing proposals for non-profit groups in Mississippi to submit for funding.

Robert participated in our first program, hosted by a black group and held in the courthouse in Grenada. When we arrived, we found the building locked for the night. The sheriff's deputies came wearing their guns and unlocked the courthouse; we filed in. Some in the audience remarked that the last time they were there they were locked up for their participation in civil rights activities.

The first professor on the program that night spoke from the judge's platform, where a railing separated the speaker from the audience. Robert was next but said, "We need to rearrange things. The speakers will move beyond the railing and join the audience." It made a tremendous difference in audience participation that night.

It was a peculiar day when Robert came into my office and said he was withdrawing from graduate school and going into politics. It was most unusual for anyone to give up a doctoral program to enter politics when the outcome of political races was always so unpredictable. He soon headed the NAACP in Mississippi and later became mayor of Vicksburg, but he was always a student and teacher of history. Robert lives by his maxim "better to fight with your mind."

Left to right: Barbara Carpenter, Joe Fant, and Cora Norman

Although the other council members during T. W.'s tenure as chair were dedicated and active, I wanted to point out some of the contributions the above members made to the introduction of public humanities programs in Mississippi.

A long-time friend of T. W. Lewis, Joseph L. Fant, was a governor appointee to the council in 1988. He was a major general with the U. S. Military Academy, West Point. With his rank, I worried about the continued camaraderie of the council but found he had a terrific sense of humor. He attended his first Federation of State Humanities Councils meeting in 1989 and reported the need for the federation to lobby for state programs. He was also in Washington, D. C. with us when Sarah Percy, a council member in the late 1970s, introduced us to her brother-in-law Walker Percy, who gave that year's Jefferson Lecture, sponsored by the NEH.

Left to right: Cora Norman, Walker Percy, and Sarah Percy.

Joe served as chair of the Screening Committee, and his resolution upon resigning from the council stated:

> The chairman of the Screening Committee requires careful reading of numerous, complex, often verbose or ambiguous proposals but also the sagacity of a fox, the wisdom of a saint and the skills of a forceful tactician in bringing this committee and the whole council to the best decisions regarding the proposals and in terms of furthering the humanities in the state of Mississippi.

He resigned after his appointment to the presidency of Marion Military Institute in Alabama; we immediately nominated him for membership on the Alabama committee.

In 1989, Lynne Cheney, chair of NEH, decided to honor ONE school teacher in each state. Those of us who labored to keep our public schools open during desegregation were appalled that Mississippi's nominee for such an award taught at a private school in Jackson. We were truly embarrassed. We initially planned to hold a joint news conference with the state superintendent of education to announce the award, but neither the MHC staff nor the State Department of Education wanted to acknowledge it.

Prior to this incident, the Phil Hardin Foundation, a significant donor, instructed us to withhold from Jackson Preparatory School any materials purchased with foundation funds because of the school's discriminatory practices. Because of the council's commitment from its inception to serve all Mississippians, the NEH award was out of sync with our policy. After the council discussed the impact of this award on their role in enhancing public education in the state, Judge Keady moved that, "The chairman be instructed to notify NEH that the award to Jackson Preparatory School was inconsistent with MHC policy of racial tolerance and against racial discrimination in any form." His motion passed unanimously, and T. W. Lewis immediately wrote a letter to Cheney explaining the consequences of such an award. We received no reply. I felt that Lynne, who grew up in Wyoming and lived for years in the East, had no idea of the commitment many of us in Mississippi made to racial tolerance. Certainly, the members of the MHC were committed to taking our programs into all communities in Mississippi.

At the next national meeting of executive directors and council chairmen in Salt Lake City, Utah, one of Cheney's staff members came to me and requested that I make sure Lewis was not at Cheney's table at dinner that night. We sat in the rear of the dining room—as far away as possible. However, when she and her husband Dick Cheney came to Pascagoula, Mississippi, in 1991 to launch a new ship, T. W. and I drove down to acknowledge her presence in our state.

Lynne Cheney no sooner left the NEH than sources quoted her as saying that Congress should eliminate the Endowment. Her statement certainly gave no value to the years I spent in Mississippi trying to mount a public humanities program with taxpayers' money.

Judge William C. Keady only served on the council for two years, from 1987 until his death in 1989, but was one of our most active members. Even though a federal judge, he attended all meetings and was most interested in the work of the MHC. He often brought Ardenia Rambeau from Mississippi Valley State University to the meetings.

Following Keady's death, T. W. Lewis appointed a committee of Carolyn Ellis Staton, chair; Rosia Crisler; Frank Riley; and Ted Alexander to make an appropriate recommendation to the council for an activity honoring Judge Keady. They recommended "A Humanities and Law Forum" on a topic to which he had given his attention, such as "Desegregation of Schools"; "Prison Reform"; or "The Tennessee Tombigbee Waterways—Environmental versus Economic Factors."

Carolyn Ellis Staton, law professor at the Ole Miss Law School, resigned from the Keady committee and the council due to family pressures. She was a full-time professor and new mother and was also in the midst of writing a book; I told her that I would even write her letter of resignation. I knew Carolyn for many years; she was a long-time voice for equality for women and my neighbor in Oxford.

Dr. Lucie Bridgforth, professor at Northwest Community College, replaced Carolyn as chair of the committee and announced the plan for Governor William Winter to speak at the first Keady Lecture in Greenville in 1990. It was a resounding success. In 1991, the Washington County Bar Association co-sponsored the second Keady Lecture, which was also in Greenville. James L. Robertson spoke on the Bill of Rights. In 1993, the Ole Miss Law School co-hosted the lecture at the University of Mississippi, and Oliver Houch addressed "Environmental Law and the Mississippi Delta Flood Plain." The MHC continues to offer the lectures in honor of Judge William C. Keady.

When Judge Keady came onto the council, his bigger-than-life reputation preceded him, and we all admitted privately that, with THIS federal judge amongst us, we must present our best faces, attempt to make erudite comments, and hide our biases. Surprisingly, we soon found him to be a warm, open, and humane colleague. Judge Keady's legal opinions contributed much to a changed Mississippi.

Imogene Borganelli served as chair of the Local Arrangements Committee for the two Keady Lectures held

in Greenville. As an advisory council member, she attended more council meetings than any other advisory member. When asked in 1993 to give her evaluation of the state-based humanities program, she stated, "MHC has been a vehicle to bind different groups together. Bonds were formed early between blacks and whites."

Imogene Borganelli

Imogene also recalled the early regrant program held in Greenville that brought a scholar from Harvard to discuss the Coleman Report on Early Childhood Education. Mississippians were honored to host a Harvard professor. After he finished his remarks concerning the Coleman Report, which stated if a child entered school disadvantaged, that child would graduate disadvantaged, Dr. Margaret Walker Alexander, one of the few blacks in the audience, got up and said, "That report is worthless and should be redone." We were all aghast at her remarks. However, years later that report was rescinded, which vindicated Dr. Alexander. She strongly believed that in education you must take a child where they are and then lift them to a higher level.

T. W. Lewis surely took a lot of "flak" while chair because I decided to run for state auditor. However, he stood beside me in my decision, supported me, and allowed me to take leave from my job and to then return to my position after my defeat. Through the years, I attended League of Women Voters' workshops on running for office, and one of the strongest recommendations was to choose the time when there was no incumbent running for reelection. Such was the case of state auditor in 1991. I asked for a leave of absence to attempt to win the election. I first called my dear friend, Ed Bishop, who was much involved in Mississippi's politics and adamant that I NOT run because it was "not a job for a woman." Undeterred, I called Eva Bishop, Ed's wife, and she said, "Go for it, and I'll support you." She did; I never knew how Ed voted. I had no political savvy and no money, but I was determined to give it a try.

The council approved my leave from July 24 through September 30, 1991, but I knew that it caused T. W. some concern. Nonetheless, he supported my leave and my candidacy. In those two months, I learned much about campaigning. At first, I wrote out my speeches but soon learned to throw the paper away and to speak from my heart. A woman cannot easily climb up on the bed of a pickup truck to make a speech holding a paper in her hand! I lost, but I remain thankful for the experience and for the council giving me unpaid leave and a job to which to return.

I was much indebted to many council and advisory council members, who helped me in the weeks that I campaigned. Charles Dunagin made speeches on my behalf in the McComb area; Katharine Rea was an ardent fund-raiser; Imogene Borganelli and Sarah Percy hosted a meeting for me in Greenville, and Boyd Golding was my constant advisor.

Samuel White, Sr. was involved for many years with the public humanities program and served on the MHC staff during one of my sabbaticals. Long before his election to membership, he took part in many MHC programs as an academic humanist while teaching at Alcorn State University. As chancery clerk in Fayette, Sam, the only Ph.D. to ever hold such an office in the state of Mississippi, brought scholarly expertise to the position. Serving on the Screening Committee, he stressed the importance of taking the humanities to the rural areas, to grassroots, to minority groups, and to generally underserved audiences.

Because I read the evaluation of every program funded while I was executive director, I say without hesitation today that the most successful program during my tenure was the Natchez Literary Conference—started in 1990, sponsored by Copiah-Lincoln Community College, and directed by Carolyn Vance Smith. They had more than one thousand attendees at that initial conference but would have been happy with one

Carolyn Vance Smith

hundred. The conference continues annually, and Carolyn does a marvelous job of offering programs of interest to scholars AND to out-of-school adults. Each year, she brings outstanding scholars to Natchez and attracts attendees from across the nation. Howell Garner, president of Copiah-Lincoln Community College, said in 2008, "This conference has helped Co-Lin, the Natchez Community, the state, and the nation for nearly 20 years. I am proud to have been a part of it since its inception. It is one of the finest things

Co-Lin has to offer." No other regrant program produced quality programs as long or as successfully as Carolyn Vance Smith's Natchez Literary Conference.

Carolyn Vance Smith
and Billy Thames

While T. W. was chair, Marjorie Berlincourt at NEH invited the two of us to help with the orientation of new council members at a meeting in Jacksonville, Florida. Several of our new council members also attended that session.

The resolution presented to T. W. as he ended his tenure as chairperson:

> Giving generously and graciously of his time, energy, and commitment to the council's many programs, to its members and staff, and to its statewide, regional, and national activities. Exemplifying the considered and courageous leadership demanded of the council in a time of frequent misunderstanding of the humanities in Mississippi and the nation. Modeling the thoughtful, temperate, and at the same time active and positive role of the humanities in

our personal, civic, and professional lives . . . T. W.
Lewis demonstrates the harmonious balance of the
man of reflection who, when he has considered an
issue and determined the proper response, pursues
that path with honesty and unflinching integrity,
bringing new life to that timeworn but appropriate
designation of gentleman and scholar. The council
has flourished under his leadership and knows that
he will continue to influence and enrich the lives
of students, colleagues, and friends, and of a wide
network of acquaintances, long after his tenure as
chair of the MHC.

The resolution also noted that he was very effective in
bringing the concerns of Mississippi to the attention of our
congressional delegation on numerous trips to Washington, D.
C., to the Federation of State Humanities Councils at national
meetings, and to the National Endowment. He was truly a
man of reflection and action, of intellect and compassion,
and above all, a man of humor and good will. T. W. Lewis

Left to right: Cora Norman, Senator Thad Cochran,
T. W. Lewis, and Barbara Carpenter.

made an incalculable contribution to the work of the MHC
and in 1998 received the Public Humanities Achievement
Award.

Left to right: T. W. Lewis, Barbara Carpenter, Representative
Jamie Whitten, Ed Bishop, and Cora Norman.

BILLY THAMES, CHAIR: 1991-1993

B illy Thames, president of Copiah-Lincoln Community College, probably became active in the Mississippi Humanities Council because of his long-time friend, Ted Alexander, whose commitment enticed Billy. He involved other community college presidents in our programs and informed Mississippi legislators of council activities.

Left to right: Ed Bishop and Billy Thames

During Lynne Cheney's tenure as chair of NEH, I learned from some of my friends at Mississippi College in Clinton that she was to speak there. I heard nothing from her office about a visit to our state, which was most unusual. However, I managed to get her arrival time and called a press conference for her at the airport. When I got to the airport, Joy Nobles, wife of the president of Mississippi College, and other women from the college were already there to meet the plane. I explained the press conference to Joy, a long-time friend. When Lynne stepped into the airport, she was unable to escape the press but was most pleasant.

In 1992, the MHC sponsored an inaugural seminar for Governor Kirk Fordice on "Civic Virtue." Although the council circulated a tape made at the pre-inaugural activities of Governor Winter, it was the first time we hosted this type of seminar. Pat Smith, professor of history at University of Southern Mississippi on the Gulf Coast, spoke on "Civic Virtue: Cato's Letters, the Founding Fathers, and the 'New Mississippi,'" and a panel made up of Clyda Rent, president of Mississippi University for Women; Barbara Holland, elementary school teacher in New Albany; T. W. Lewis; and Lucie Bridgforth followed.

Smith was outstanding in bringing the humanities to Mississippians of all ages, interests, and educational levels. As a project director, he sponsored one of the MHC's most successful programs, a conference on global education which drew plaudits from teachers, scholars, public officials, and the general public alike. It also claimed one of our largest audiences. Governor Mabus opened the conference, and Hodding Carter, son of Greenville's newspaper editor, participated from Washington through a teleconference hook up. We later replicated that program in northern Mississippi.

Pat took part in the MHC programs funded to enhance the teaching of social studies as well as programs that televised discussions of contested values. He attended a special meeting with the Kettering Foundation to discuss the public role of the scholar, a role he exemplified.

Lucie Bridgforth chaired the initial Keady Lecture, coordinated the MHC programs at Northwest Mississippi Community College with the DeSoto County Historical Society, and was project director for the Scholar-in-Residence program in DeSoto County. Her distinguished brother Justice James L. Robertson, featured speaker at the second Keady Lecture, often escorted her to council gatherings.

One outstanding program that Lucie directed at Northwest focused on farmers, who faced changing economic conditions, new farm technology, and governmental regulations. Many invested their lives in farming and found that they could not sustain or, for some, even keep their farms. They felt it was a personal failure. Out of that program, they began to see that they were caught up in a national as well as a state dilemma. Experts explained that as our economy became more global everyone would have to make adjustments. Realizing they faced obstacles over which they had no control, the local farmers left feeling better about themselves.

Barbara Holland participated in the governor's inaugural seminar in honor of Governor Kirk Fordice and spoke on "Educating Our Children for Civic Responsibilities in the New Millennium." She also represented the council at a meeting at the Kettering Foundation and returned home to give a rousing speech, "We Need Active Scholars!" When we hosted the 1994 Southern Regional Humanities Councils, Barbara served as tour guide aboard a bus en route to the Natchez Literary Conference and entertained her group by discussing Mississippi writers. She was an early project director for the MHC funded programs directed at school children and involved her elementary students in New Albany in their local history. They recorded spot announcements for a local radio station from their research findings and later presented them as a program directed by Barbara—most memorable.

Macy Hart, long-time enthusiast for Jewish history in Mississippi, was involved from the early days of the council and was most instrumental in establishing the Museum of the Southern Jewish Experience in Utica. In 1992, a multicultural workshop for teachers was held at that museum.

At the March 1993 council meeting, I made the following comments concerning Billy's involvement:

> I must acknowledge the time and commitment the chair continues to give to the activities of the Mississippi Humanities Council. He is always present despite his own hectic schedule as president of Copiah-Lincoln Community College. We have had outstanding chairs always—all have stood out on the national scene. BUT, we have never had a chair who worked harder than Billy Thames to promote the MHC and tell academicians, legislators, and civic leaders of the import of the MHC program on this state.

When his tenure as chair ended, Billy's resolution stated:

> . . . [He] became an immediate convert and enthusiastic participant, attending board meetings and regrant programs alike and preaching the humanities to new audiences and constituents; lending his reputation for absolute integrity to the activities of the council; attending regional and national meetings; mounting a personal crusade with the Mississippi legislature; successfully negotiating

to establish a role in gubernatorial inaugurals for the Mississippi Humanities Council.

Billy Thames received much recognition for his leadership—from the National Endowment for the Humanities, Phi Theta Kappa with the Mosal Award for Distinguished Alumnus, and most importantly, from his own board of trustees for twenty-five distinguished years of service to his college. He visited Germany as a guest of the Carl Duisberg Society and met with German educators. In 1996, Billy received the Public Humanities Achievement Award by the MHC.

JEANNE LUCKETT, CHAIR: 1993-1994

Jeanne Luckett

The council elected Jeanne Luckett chairperson of the Mississippi Humanities Council in December 1993, but she became a member in 1990 and was involved in humanities programs almost from the very beginning. In the first years of the council's existence, she prepared a multi-media production on children for an early statewide conference and salvaged a production of "Who, What, and Where" with ETV. Jeanne helped with auditions for the first Mississippi Chautauqua, prepared pro bono the MHC's 1992 fundraising prospectus, presided over the 1993 press conference with NEH Chair Lynne Cheney, and attended regional and national meetings representing the council. In 1992, she was elected to the Executive Committee of the Southern Regional Media Fund.

Jeanne worked tirelessly while chair of the MHC to polish its image and keep it before the public. She demonstrated Mississippi's hospitality while hosting the 1994 Southern Regional Humanities Councils meeting and presided with grace at the Scholars Conference in Olive Branch in 1994.

Dr. Gemma Beckley, professor of social work at Rust College, was involved in the humanities program long before she became a member of the council in 1994. My friendship with her began before any of my other ongoing friendships, and she provided continuous support while I was executive director.

Standing, left to right: Gemma Beckley and Katharine Rea. *Seated:* Cora Norman.

Gemma helped plan programs on term limits with the MHC and the Secretary of State's Office. A referendum on term limits was slated to be on the ballot, and rather than sponsor a pro or con program, humanities professors presented both advantages and disadvantages in one program. There were two factions over this issue, and tempers flared throughout the state. I feared there would be trouble at the first meeting, held at Itawamba Community College, so I called President Cole. He and all his deans were there, as well as the campus police, but all was quiet.

In 1993, Phi Theta Kappa selected me to participate on a panel at their national conference in Dallas on "Diversity versus Unity." As a member since 1944, I was honored to be on their national program. Rod Risley, head of the organization, was a great supporter of our work and later joined the MHC and served as chair after I retired.

The meeting in Dallas gave me an opportunity to spend some time with Doug Foard, who was at the National Endowment for the Humanities before he became executive director of Phi Beta Kappa. He visited us in Mississippi several times while with the NEH, and it was I who brought the heads of Phi Theta Kappa and Phi Beta Kappa together long before the Dallas conference. On one of my many trips to Washington, D. C., I set up a meeting with Doug and Rod in a local bar; it seemed that I conducted all serious business in bars. They

Left to right: Cora Norman, Charles Lowery, and Doug Foard.

immediately became friends, and Rod involved Doug in several of his national and international meetings of Phi Theta Kappa.

David Dunbar, who served on the council while Jeanne was chair, was very active in council activities and was a strong advocate for our funds going to community programs rather than to universities and colleges. Today, I wonder if that would have changed the impact of our program.

LESLIE BURL MCLEMORE, CHAIR: 1994-1996

Leslie McLemore and Cora Norman

Dr. Leslie McLemore, professor of political science at Jackson State University, probably participated in more humanities' programs than any other professor in Mississippi. In the early days, the proposal writers sought him when they needed a black on their program. I remain very indebted to him for his participation in those early days and for staying with the program through the years.

Les became a member of the Mississippi Humanities Council in 1990 and became chair in 1994. He pointed out the need to appoint spouses of key legislators to membership on the council. Because he was involved for many years in the state-based program, he recognized the need to keep our legislators informed and felt that spouses would help in that regard.

The Federation of State Humanities Councils recognized Les' leadership and elected him to their board in 1995. The board then elected him vice president and appointed him to their committee to select a new president. He was influential in the choice of Gayle Leftwich, who replaced long-time president, Jamil Zainaldin. Gayle later visited us in Mississippi.

Left to right: Leslie McLemore, Cora Norman, Senator Thad Cochran, and Cindy Phillips.

When Gayle left, Esther Mackintosh, who was part of the federation for many years, became president. Several of us formed a support group and got together when possible, and Esther was part of that group; others included Alice Barkley, executive director of North Carolina; Robert Cheatham, executive director of Tennessee; and Chuck Daugherty, executive director from West Virginia.

Following the meeting of the Southern Regional Humanities Councils in Mississippi in 1994, Chuck, Alice, Esther, and I made our way to the Gulf Coast. Aubrey Lucas, president at University of Southern Mississippi, gave me permission to use the president's cottage on the USM campus at Long

Beach, Mississippi. The cottage had only one bedroom, so we gave it to Chuck. Esther and Alice took a bed in the dining room, and I took the couch. I never told Aubrey about the man in our midst. But after one night in the cottage, we took Chuck to the airport and saw him off to West Virginia, where he was to marry the next day.

The same group gathered for a weekend in Alice's condo on the East Coast, and later, Esther and I visited Alice in her home in Greensboro. At Alice's retirement celebration, Bob Young, former executive director of Arizona, Esther, and I made our way to North Carolina for the occasion. In retirement, I truly miss those close relationships with my national colleagues.

Left to right: Cora Norman, Alice Barkley, Chuck Daugherty, and Esther Mackintosh.

Left to right: Chuck Daugherty, Cora Norman, and Alice Barkley.

Left to right: Esther Mackintosh and Alice Barkley.

Dr. Melerson Guy Dunham, retired from Alcorn State University, had a number of early regrants for programs at Prentiss Institute and always had Dr. Leslie McLemore and Dr. Peggy Prenshaw on her programs. She reported that Les zoomed up at the exact opening minute in his little German Porsche, performed his job eloquently, and then waved goodbye from his Porsche. Thirty years later, I believe he still has that car.

On the eve of the conference for business leaders held at the Mississippi Power and Light Lodge in Jackson in 1975, I drove to Jackson to meet our guest speaker from Utah. Les and his brother, Eugene, went with me to the airport and planned to go out to dinner with us. I asked him to take us some place where we could get soul food. During my early visits in the black communities, I heard much about soul food and was curious. Leslie took us to a restaurant, and to my amazement, I found that soul food was the same food I, a southerner, grew up on and loved all my life—greens, yams, butterbeans!

Under Leslie's leadership, the council elected some of our long-time supporters to membership. Since they were involved for years, they brought an abundance of knowledge and support to the council.

Barbara Dease was long involved in public humanities programs prior to her membership on the council. She helped me get language teachers involved in the program in the early years and in 1995 suggested we invite colleges and universities to send representatives to the annual awards banquet to identify their young scholars. It certainly made the attendance at the banquet much larger and more representative of the state.

Left to right: Barbara Dease and Cora Norman

Jack Rogers came onto the council as I retired but was involved in many of our programs as a history professor. For many years at any statewide meeting, the three history graduates from Ole Miss were always together—Jack, Jan Hawks, and Carey Hearn. They were a close team.

Another historian, who served about the same time on the MHC, was Ellis Woolfolk Darby, our voice in Tunica and a great lover of Mississippi history. One of the state office buildings in Jackson, the Woolfolk Building, was named for Ellis' great-grandfather.

Another very early supporter of the state-based humanities program, Troy Holliday became a member of the council in my last days with the MHC. He was county superintendent of Tippah County when I first met him. A building at Northeast Community College bears his name because of his contributions to education. Troy was always available when called, and I enjoyed working with him.

Alpha Morris from Alcorn State University, involved in the program long before she came onto the council, participated in almost all of the programs funded at her university. In my last days as executive director, I experienced my first displeasure from one or two of the council members, but I always knew that Alpha supported me! She had an unusual

Left to right: Alpha Morris and Cora Norman.

tenure with the council—ten years!—and in 2005 received the MHC's Public Humanities Achievement Award.

I was distraught over the displeasure of two members but also knew that I had great support on the council from Jack White from Mississippi State University. His wife Emilie was our staff person at MSU, and Jack, who participated in many of our programs, accompanied Emilie whenever she attended a regrant program. He was a welcomed professor in the black community, and in 2003 the council awarded Jack its Humanities Scholar Award.

Cora Norman and Jack White

Another great supporter through the years, who finally became a member of the council, was Vivian Presley, president of Coahoma Community College. Even with her presidential duties, she found time to attend council meetings.

John Hampton Stennis, son of Senator John Stennis, was in the audience of many regrant programs long before he became a member of the council, even though he was a busy lawyer. It was always a happy experience to see John

Hampton, and his presence gave credibility to the program. While Sheldon Hackney was chairman of NEH, he came to Mississippi to attend our first awards ceremony in 1994. I also scheduled an interview for him with Mississippi ETV prior to the awards ceremony. Following the ceremony, we had a reception.

Cora Norman and Sheldon Hackney.

Left to right: Don Cotton, Sheldon Hackney, and Cora Norman.

Left to right: Leslie McLemore, Brenda Gray, Celia Booth, and Ed Bishop.

Left to right: Jack Bass, Governor William Winter, Billy Thames, and Sheldon Hackney.

Left to right: Robert Walker, Celia Booth, Peggy Prenshaw, and Cora Norman.

Left to right: Governor William Winter, Ellis Darby, Ed Bishop, Luther Munford, Barbara Holland and Peggy Prenshaw.

I met Sheldon Hackney when he was president of Tulane University in New Orleans, Louisiana. He attended a meeting on the Mississippi Gulf Coast concerning the Equal Rights Amendment and women. Years later, I found in my files a letter from Mr. Gilbert Vorhoff, a banker from New Orleans, who also attended that meeting with Sheldon. I worked hard for the passage of the ERA, and I was delighted when I found Vorhoff's letter to me:

Just a note to say how much I enjoyed being with
you in Biloxi, and how impressed I was with your
intelligence and your lucid (albeit prejudiced)
arguments in support of the ERA. You *almost* had
me convinced.

I also wanted to thank you for inviting me to your
cocktail party and to the dinner at Frenchie's. I hope
you'll give me the opportunity to reciprocate by
inviting you to dinner with 13 men some evening in
New Orleans.

I replied:

I appreciate your kind note. However, I am fully
aware that even after my argument in support of ERA
you voted against it. Therefore, my task is unfinished,
and I look forward to another chance with you.

Anytime I have the opportunity to have dinner in
New Orleans with 13 *intelligent,* mature men I shall
be happy to accept.

I must admit the invitation never came. Perhaps, there were
not 13 intelligent, mature men on Vorhoff's list. Sadly,
Mississippi was the only state that never considered the ERA
on the floor of their legislature. The bill never got out of the
committee to which it was assigned.

We long recognized the need for a media person as Charles
Dunagin, editor of McComb's *Enterprise-Journal*, left the
council in 1984. After I announced my retirement, Will
Sullivan summed up the council's activities and wrote a very
congratulatory newspaper article.

Governor Kirk Fordice appointed Cindy Phillips to the council. She was a steadfast Republican, and I was—and remain—a devoted Democrat, but we had a great relationship. We roomed together on a trip to Washington, D. C., and I found her to be a wonderful roommate. Although my association with Cindy was rather brief, she had a long tenure on the council.

The following was one of my later charges to the MHC at its "Planning and Assessment Meeting":

> As you plan programs for the future, we know that there are many ills in our state which the humanities can not address. However, the humanities can deal with values which are at the core of our society—compassion, honor, tolerance, self respect, curiosity—as well as with knowledge of history, and the capacity to think creatively about the future. These are values which are at the root of individual and civic lives. We know that material things are important. We need material things, and we all actively strive for them. But when you add up all the things in the world, what you have are a bunch of things. It is MEANING, it is the intangible world of values, the spiritual dimension of ultimate beliefs that give the material world true content. As we move into the 21stcentury, the questions and demands in the public arena can only become more intense, and we are going to need all of the tools at our disposal for coping and staying together. One of those tools, the humanities, is our business. As we try to explain the humanities, we talk much about disciplines, texts, museum exhibits, even film. To me, in the public humanities program, the humanities are a "DISCOURSE," a conversation

with others in the community around ideas or values, thoughts and knowledge. As creators and as participants, the humanities belong to all of us.

In 1994, the MHC funded a scholars meeting in Olive Branch, Mississippi. One member of the council was very critical of that meeting and afterwards said that it should never have been funded. However, we claimed more community college professors for that meeting than ever before. I really appreciated the letter from Ovid Vickers, professor of literature at East Central Community College, following that Olive Branch meeting:

> . . . I just wanted to let you know what a worthwhile meeting it was. To realize the importance of a meeting of that kind one must have time to reflect on what transpired.

> The value of the meeting, as I see it, was threefold. The most worthwhile aspect was the opportunity to exchange ideas with teachers and others from across Mississippi. So much was gained from conversations in the hallways, at lunch, waiting for a session to begin, and yes, at tables in the lounge. Secondly, we have a tendency to think that all Mississippians think alike and have the same problems statewide. The meeting proved otherwise. What is of great importance to a teacher in North Mississippi may not be considered worthy of attention by one who teaches on the Gulf Coast. A third factor was the bringing together of those who instruct in the Senior Institutions with those from the Community Colleges. Seeming differences have always existed there, and

> this meeting certainly went a long way in bridging the gap, imagined or real, between these two groups.
>
> I found the meeting to be a delightful social experience, and at the same time some very challenging and thought provoking ideas were presented. Your efforts to bring together the people, ideas, and institutions present at this meeting certainly speak well for your continued efforts to make the Mississippi Humanities Council a contributing factor in the improvement of life and learning in Mississippi.

Ovid Vickers received the MHC's Chair's Award for Special Achievements in the Humanities in 2003.

In 1994, I received Mississippi State University's "Outstanding Mississippi Woman's" award. Undoubtedly, they based the award as much on my contributions toward improving the status of women as on my work with the state humanities program.

As I looked back, I recognized that programs that dealt with controversial topics claimed larger audiences and that those citizens who came and expected hot debate found, instead, "reasoned discourse" with many opinions expressed. It was this track record that led the Secretary of State's Office to turn to the MHC in 1995 to host public forums on "Term Limits." It was no easy challenge to deal with an organized group that came with the determination that only one side be aired.

In 1995, we were able to attract Ernest Boyer, well known American educator with the Carnegie Foundation, to the state. The Phil Hardin Foundation provided funds for us to print and distribute his speech, "What Is an Educated Person?" He dealt with history, language, civics, and our responsibility to search urgently for our commonalities as well—"It's true that all people are different. But it's also true that we're all connected to the planet Earth, and to be truly educated for the next century means understanding our connectedness to nature."

When the NEH named Dr. Peggy Prenshaw, former University of Southern Mississippi professor, a 1994 Charles Frankel Scholar, all Mississippi scholars received a boost for participating in the public humanities program. Near the end of my work with the council, I found that professors asked me to write letters of recommendation when they sought deanships of colleges of liberal arts as well as tenureship, so the perception of academic credibility of state humanities programs certainly rose through the years. The involvement and support of the presidents of community and junior colleges in MHC's activities evidenced the respect of academic institutions.

Peggy Prenshaw with Family and Cora Norman *far right.*

President and Mrs. Bill Clinton, and Peggy Prenshaw.

My last efforts to involve a community were in Bogue Chitto. We had one or two programs there, but I never felt we succeeded in bringing representatives from the black and white communities together. However, after my retirement, I received a letter from Johnny Washington, a leader in the black community in Bogue Chitto, "in appreciation for services rendered to our community educational program in 1996."

We were grateful for the support we received from Carole Watson, our liaison until Lynne Cheney moved her to the chairman's office. Jessie Mosley hosted Carole at our meeting in Tupelo when she visited Mississippi. She wanted to see Elvis Presley's home, and Jessie took her there while in Tupelo. We had many telephone calls with Carole and visited with her in Washington. Even when she moved to Chairman Cheney's office, we knew we could always call her for advice.

ton was in the White House, I joined the forces
President to name Bill Ferris as chairman of
to President Clinton:

5 August 1997

linton

20500

airman of the National
ent for the Humanities

nton:

etter is to endorse the recommendation of Dr.
the University of Mississippi for the new
H. Bill has served as an outstanding Director
the Study of Southern Culture at the University
of Mississippi. He would do a good job at NEH.

I was the first Executive Director of the Mississippi
Humanities Council and served for 24 years. retiring last year.
During that time I worked under a number of NEH Chairmen. The
academicians have always demanded a recognized "scholar" for this
position. However, it has been my observation that we need a
person who understands what the humanities contribute to everyday
living and has the added ability to tell the Congress what a
knowledge of the humanities contributes to a person's citizenship!
Bill Ferris is a recognized scholar. I believe that he can also
work with the Congress.

Being a southerner (from Arkansas) I hang my head in
shame today when I recall how embarrassed I was when my uncle
visited me at Magnolia A & M College (now Southern Arkansas
University) in the 1940s not in his Sunday School clothes but in
his overalls! Bill Ferris has helped me to understand what our
families in overalls did to preserve our Southland and the
valuable contributions they made to our lives. They valued
family, education and instilled in us the dignity of work. They
knew the value of humans helping other humans in the time of need.
This understanding of our heritage is part of the humanities.
Bill Ferris has helped Southerners to appreciate their heritage.
Bill Ferris can help to instill human dignity to the challenges at
NEH.

Please give Dr. Bill Ferris your serious consideration
for Chairman of the National Endowment for the Humanities (and use
your clout to increase the appropriation to NEH).

Sincerely,

Cora Norman

The President appointed Ferris chairman of the NEH, and he served from 1997 until 2001. His work with the legislators was outstanding. Senator Jesse Helms from North Carolina opposed the humanities appropriation for several years, but apparently he and Bill became friends. We certainly heard no opposition from Helms while Ferris was chairman.

In January 1996, I announced my retirement from the council effective June 1, 1996. At that meeting, I noted the many opportunities and challenges I had as executive director since 1972 and appreciated the support I received from the council members through the years. The council held a reception in December, and at that time, Leslie McLemore announced the establishment of the Norman Lecture.

Leslie Myers, from *The Clarion-Ledger* in Jackson, interviewed me shortly before I retired and asked what I thought we accomplished with the public humanities program:

> It has given me a vehicle to bring different cultures together to discuss in a civil way, with civility— instead of shooting each other, fighting each other, cursing each other, or not even talking to each other, and that's been my bag. People are my bag.

I retired while Les was chair of the MHC. My last meeting was in Natchez, and my long-time friends, Katharine Rea and Imogene Borganelli, were both there with me. At the council meeting that day, Imogene said, "I appreciated the opportunity to serve on the council. The Mississippi Humanities Council has been a blessing to the state." That night we had our own get-together at the bar, and they presented me a ring. What friends they were. Katharine died in 2005, and Imogene has become even dearer to me.

My Last Council Meeting, Natchez. *Left to right:* Leslie McLemore, Mayor Butch Brown, Governor William Winter, Billy Thames, Senator Thad Cochran, and Cora Norman.

Left to right: Cora Norman, Katharine Rea, and Imogene Borganelli.

The contributions of the Mississippi Humanities Council to the state of Mississippi are vast. Danny McKenzie's article, "Historian Says 21st Century Is Mississippi's Century," in Tupelo's *Northeast Mississippi Daily Journal,* February 6, 2000, acknowledged those contributions and quoted David Sansing of the University of Mississippi:

> While there have been many organizations and agencies in recent years that have provided for this Mississippi great awakening, Sansing says the Mississippi Humanities Council is among the most important groups, among the most significant groups.
>
> "They have been one of the major forces during the past 30 years in shaping our state and its culture," he says. "They were begun in 1970 and since then they have been one of the most positive forces to ever work in Mississippi. They put on programs all over Mississippi where black citizens and white citizens came together in a spirit of celebration, and each of our races found out there is much to be celebrated in Mississippi."

And, Sansing says, it is still that way, more than ever.
To which we must all add, "Amen."

I know that Les McLemore was instrumental in establishing the Cora Norman Lecture Series and in planning the December reception in honor of my retirement. The reception was a memorable evening for me as many of my friends went to the microphone and gave me accolades. It was also nice to have Edie Manza, MHC's liaison with NEH, with us for that evening.

Left to right: Aubrey Lucas, David Beckley, and Gerald Turner.

Left to right: Norma Fields, John Stennis, and Lucie
Bridgforth.

Left to right: Rod Risley, Bill Jones, Aubrey Lucas, and Kathryn Jones.

Left to right: Tom Flynn and Glenn Watts.

Left to right: Edie Manza and
Cora Norman.

My friendship with Leslie McLemore is long and continuous. He is a man that I have admired and loved through the years, and I am indebted to him for his help with humanities programs and our many social gatherings in which he was the central figure. Whenever I planned a group get-together, he was involved. In 2002, the MHC awarded Leslie McLemore the Humanities Educator Award.

In retirement, I miss the contacts I had with groups and individuals throughout Mississippi as well as my national colleagues through annual meetings of the Federation of State Humanities Councils.

MY EIGHT WOMEN: "AGENTS OF CHANGE IN MISSISSIPPI DURING THE TWENTIETH CENTURY"

From almost every perspective, events of the twentieth century transformed women's lives in Mississippi. Whether it was in the area of women's suffrage, education, civil rights, and/or economic status, women involved themselves in the issues and made the difference. In the early 1990s, I began to contemplate women who were change agents in their own eras. Each person, no doubt, would have their own list of women change agents, but I chose eight Mississippi women of the twentieth century, four black and four white, who made a difference in our state with their courage, willingness, and commitment to speak out for the equality of women and the dignity of the human being.

The Gulf Coast chapter of the American Association of University Women invited me to speak on these women agents of change after hearing of my research. I drove down early to spend the evening prior to the speech with my dear friend and mentor, Katharine Rea. Katharine knew that she was one of my agents and refused to attend the meeting. The next day she changed her mind and went with me, but she excused herself prior to my speech. She was always generous in acknowledging others, but had great difficulty hearing accolades for herself.

Younger women today seem unaware of the struggles that some women of long ago faced and survived, giving future generations their rights. Yesterday, as women, their majors in higher education were limited to those men felt appropriate; today, women have access to all areas of higher education, including medicine and engineering.

We were at Ole Miss a long time before a female enrolled in the college of engineering. I recalled that Judge Mary Libby Payne's mother said she wanted to study mathematics when she went to the University of Mississippi. Being a woman, she had to appeal to every faculty member at the university for consent to major in mathematics. She graduated at the head of her class.

Women had no credit cards; today credit cards are mailed without college students asking for them. Even when we finally got credit cards with our names on them, we found that the account numbers on our cards were our husbands' numbers. We had no credit rating for loans. I had a Ph.D., was a graduate of Harvard's Institute for Management, and headed an office at the R & D Building in Jackson, but the bank refused my request for a $2000 loan because I had no credit rating.

After retiring from the Mississippi Humanities Council, I listed the speech on my eight women change agents in MHC's Speakers Bureau. Four of the women were very much involved in the state humanities programs—Margaret Walker Alexander, Katharine Rea, Jessie Mosley, and Frances Coleman.

Because of some earlier women, often seen as obnoxious, our younger women no longer fight the same battles. The twentieth century began with a crusade for women's suffrage and ended with women choosing their own career paths.

Some went into the corporate world, and in 2008, a woman made a strong bid for the presidency.

My eight women who stood up for women's rights and opportunities: Nellie Nugent Somerville, who led the fight in Mississippi for women to vote and was the first woman elected to the Mississippi House of Representatives; Fannie Lou Hamer, who changed the Democratic Party in Mississippi; Margaret Walker Alexander, our outspoken scholar who wrote "For My People"; Winson Hudson, who stood up in her community and filed a school desegregation suit against the state; Jessie Mosley, who founded the Smith Robertson Museum in Jackson; Jean Muirhead, who obtained the right for women to serve on juries in Mississippi; Katharine Rea, who worked with women throughout the state; and Frances Coleman, who helped pave the way at Mississippi State University for recognition of women. All of these women stood out as activists in their day.

Nellie Nugent Somerville

Nellie Nugent Somerville lived in Greenville. She adamantly rejected the prevailing view from the 1880s thru the 1920s that women should confine their activities and influence to their homes and families. Nellie was inspired to work for increasing women's influence in politics by Frances Willard, president of the national Women Christian Temperance Movement (WCTU). Nellie became corresponding secretary for the state WCTU in 1896. She initially declined to work for suffrage, saying she was "up to my eyes in WCTU work, to say nothing of family." However, in 1897 she gave up her WCTU post to become the president of the Mississippi Women Suffrage Association. She resigned as president of MWSA in 1899, and Belle Kearney took over the role. But the association was dormant until 1906, when Kearney and Somerville revived interest. It continued to be a force in the state, regional, and national suffrage organizations until the movement ended with the ratification of the 19th Amendment in 1920. Mississippi refused women the vote in the 1920 election and waited until 1984 to ratify the amendment!

Women voted for the first time in Mississippi in the 1923 election. Nellie Nugent Somerville was elected to the state legislature, barely ahead of fellow suffrage leader Belle Kearney, who was elected to the Mississippi Senate later the same year. Mrs. Somerville served in the Senate until 1927. There, she chaired the Committee on Eleemosynary Institutions, led the way for major reforms in the state's mental hospital—moving the hospital to Whitfield, sponsored the bill establishing Delta State Teacher's College, and served as a delegate to the Democratic National Convention in 1924.

She consistently signed her name Nellie Nugent Somerville, not Mrs. Robert Somerville. When my husband and I moved to Columbia, South Carolina, in 1959, the bank we selected for the deposit of our meager funds insisted I use Mrs. William Norman on our account rather than Cora Norman as I wished. I persisted, not knowing at that time that I was a feminist, and won that fight.

Nellie opposed liquor, opposed integration of the races, and promoted the poll tax. Years after Nellie left the political scene, I found that I disagreed with her stand on all three issues. However, I felt indebted to her for working for the right of women to vote.

I recalled visiting her daughter, my mentor Lucy Somerville Howorth, at Nellie's house in Mount Eagle, Tennessee. Although Nellie died years before, Lucy still honored her mother's memory. When I got up to go get Lucy the bottle of wine I brought to her, she said to me, "Don't you let anyone see you bring that wine into this house." Nellie Nugent's portrait now hangs in the Mississippi Hall of Fame. I nominated Lucy Somerville Howorth for the Mississippi Hall of Fame but was unsuccessful. Nellie Nugent Somerville was also included in *Mississippi Women: Their Histories: Their Lives* edited by Martha Swain, Elizabeth Anne Payne, and Marjorie Spruill (2003).

Fannie Lou Hamer

Fannie Lou Hamer became a beacon of light in the hearts of countless Americans of all colors. The youngest of twenty children, this woman of the soil dared to dream and emerged as a doer and visionary of the highest order. Her life certainly impacted politics in Mississippi. During her formative years in Sunflower County, Fannie Lou acquired very little formal schooling. She went to school after the harvesting season— four months a year in a one-room shack on a Sunflower County plantation. However, blessed with a sharp analytical mind, Fannie Lou Hamer was able to use her limited formal education in a positive manner.

She was a leader on the various plantations before becoming involved in the civil rights movement. In 1962, when she attempted to register to vote, the Marlow Plantation evicted her for resisting the status quo. Only two years later, the heroics of Mrs. Hamer at the 1964 Democratic National Convention in Atlantic City shook the conscience of white Americans. That single event, her testimony before the Credentials Committee describing the attack on her in Winona, Mississippi, where the police beat her, started a movement that was to have a profound impact upon America. Her testimony was so effective that President Lyndon Johnson called a press conference to divert the country's attention. His gambit failed, for Fannie Lou's story caught the attention of the American people. Her testimony was so powerful that the Mississippi Freedom Democratic Party's claim of being the legitimate delegation from Mississippi had renewed credence. The recital of her sadistic beating by Mississippi police tore at the veil that concealed the brutality of life in the South. Calls and telegrams poured into the convention and stirred the delegates into an historic decision; they invited two members of the Freedom Democratic Party to be seated at-large for the first time in history, and a major party pledged in the future to refuse to honor any delegation that was not democratically chosen. I was ignorant of the fact that white men beat black women during the civil rights fight until I read Unita Blackwell's book *Barefootin'* (2006).

In addition to moving the people with her speeches, she sang the gospel song "Go Tell It on The Mountain," the lyrics of which encouraged believers to tell of a new day, a new joy on the horizon. For Hamer, this new day was about economic empowerment for black people in Mississippi. Her legacy was showing us how to live with pain and challenge. In that regard, the abstract meaning of her story was not about triumph or defeat but how best to live life with what one has, forever priming oneself to push for a bit more; one person CAN make a difference! Fannie Lou was frequently quoted: "I'm sick and tired of being sick and tired. You can pray until you faint, but if you do not get up and do something, God is not going to put it into your lap."

After the Atlantic City Convention, Fannie Lou Hamer challenged the Mississippi Congressional delegation, traveled to Africa, ran for the Mississippi Senate, and established several self-help projects in Sunflower County and the surrounding area. In 1997, Leslie Burl McLemore implemented the Fannie Lou Institute on Citizenship and Democracy at Jackson State University to continue telling the story of Fannie Lou Hamer's struggles.

Margaret Walker Alexander

Margaret Walker Alexander was a professor of literature at Jackson State University for many years and founded the Institute for the Study of History, Life, and Culture of Black People, renamed in 1990 The Margaret Walker Alexander National Research Center for the Study of the 20th Century African American in her honor. She was an outstanding teacher, a scholar, a writer, an active and civic-minded citizen, and an activist. Unlike many literary writers, she was also a community person. Her works included the classic poem "For My People," the book of the same title which won the Yale Younger Poets Award, the novel *Jubilee,* the biography of her novelist friend from the 1930s *Richard Wright, Daemoniac Genius, A_Portrait of the Man*, and her collected poems *This IS My Century.*

In 1976, Morgan State University awarded Dr. Margaret Walker Alexander an honorary degree of doctor of humane letters with the following citation:

> In the struggle for black liberation few have stood longer in ranks than Margaret Walker Alexander. She has been the voice of hope when days were dark; the voice of praise for victories won. No matter the medium, whether novel, short story, or poem, her words have been produced, as she herself has written For My People everywhere.

I met Margaret at our first regrant program in Greenville, hosted by a predominantly white civic group. Their speaker was from Harvard and talked about the Coleman Report, which maintained that if a child entered school disadvantaged, he or she would graduate from school disadvantaged. There were few blacks in that audience in the early 1970s, yet Margaret stood up and loudly said, "That report is not worth the paper it is written on. You go back and redo that report." We listened. Years later, I heard that another report came out of Harvard and supported Margaret's philosophy that a good teacher takes a student where they are and lifts them up.

Alex and Margaret Walker Alexander

Dr. Alexander knew every major black writer in America during the twentieth century and most of the minor ones. Her list of friends, colleagues, and admirers spanned the nation and reached into other countries. In 1973, she planned and administered the Phyllis Wheatley Poetry Festival, which brought to Jackson State University many of the outstanding black—and some white—writers who were also her personal friends. She received funds from the Mississippi Humanities Council for that conference.

Margaret Alexander was a role model for her people. She wrote for them and gave inspiration and hope to many persons who had little inspiration and even less for which to hope. I was appreciative for her friendship and for letters she wrote on my behalf as I sought professional advancement. She taught me something about being a mentor. She was also an outstanding cook. She prided herself with her fruitcakes at Thanksgiving, using her grandmother Vrylie's recipe. One year, she invited me to her house for an afternoon get-together with only her and Eudora Welty to enjoy her fruitcake. We spent several hours in her kitchen/dining room, and I had no camera and made no notes. How stupid can one be?

Margaret was on many of our early humanities programs—
far more than Eudora Welty. She was not only known in
the state, but spoke at locations throughout the nation. She
feared flying, so her husband Alex drove her.

In 2004, I attended a national Women's Meeting in Pretoria,
South Africa. The mayor of Pretoria welcomed the group
and even in his short presentation quoted from Margaret's
"For My People."

I served on the board of the Margaret Walker Alexander
Research Institute at Jackson State University for several
years. I was vice chair and often presided at our meetings
because the chair was Dr. Robert Smith, a medical doctor.
Moving from Mississippi, I remained on the board. Because
of Margaret Walker Alexander's influence on the black
culture, I maintained that every student graduating from
Jackson State University needed at least one seminar on her
contributions.

Left to right: Cora Norman, Donna Godwin, and
Margaret Walker Alexander.

Winson Hudson

Winson Hudson was one of 14 children. Large families were very protective of their children, especially girls. If white men caught a girl alone, they often raped her, but parents were afraid to say anything for fear the Ku Klux Klan might visit that night. Winson said, "When the KKK would come into our community, other people would come to our house, for Daddy was not afraid, and that taught us."

Visiting the Women's Portrait Gallery in Washington, D. C., I saw her portrait hanging in the gallery. I returned to Mississippi determined to meet her. I discovered that my long-time friend, George Williams, was from Harmony Community near Carthage, Mississippi, and related to Ms. Hudson. He drove me to Harmony Community to meet her in her home. I found the walls of her front room covered with plaques and pictures of her activities. I discovered also that earlier she spoke throughout the United States about civil rights activities in Mississippi but many, many of our white citizens in Mississippi knew nothing about her.

George Williams and Winson Hudson.

Winson Hudson and Cora Norman.

Winson told me that when a petition circulated for the school board to desegregate the public schools, she signed it. Officials pressured whites to remove their names. She had borrowed a little bit of money from the bank to plant her crop, but the banker then called her in and said, "We've been mighty good to you; we lent you money." She replied, "But I've been paying it back, haven't I?" The banker countered, "But we have to have our money now, or else we're going to foreclose." She said she wasn't going to remove her name from the petition, "You'll just have to foreclose. My seven cows and one mule are there when you get ready to pick 'em up." Winson told me, "The more they did to us, the meaner we got. Our husbands were not as brave as we were. We had to protect our men. If my husband had've been in my place, he would not have made it, cause the black man has always been the target."

Hudson's account of registering to vote had to be included here; I hope that our younger women will remember her story when they go to register. Her account:

> One time we went into the courthouse, and we saw a bunch of great big ol' white men clustered around the door where we had to go in and register. I say, "Dovie [Dovie was Winson's sister], they got us today." She said, "Let's go down in the basement and pray." We went down in the basement, and she prayed. They said I was too mean to pray. Dovie talked to the Lord about it. And she said, "Let's go. There's a shield over us. They can't touch us." So we walked way down the long hall. They had the door covered and were clustered around. And do you know we walked through those men and just rubbed 'em. "Excuse me, excuse me." And they just turned their backs.

When we went in to register, they would come and
put a card down. It was just big enough for two eyes.
It said, "The eyes of the Klan are upon you. You have
been identified by the White Knights of the Ku
Klux Klan."

When we went in to register, they gave you a sheet of
paper and an article in the Mississippi Constitution.
When you get through writing it, then you got to
interpret it. And so you do all of this. And then I'd
go back, and they'd say, "The board said y'all didn't
pass." I'd say, "What board?" "Well, we got a board
and they said y'all didn't pass." And we'd go back
again.

A lawyer from the Justice Department came here and
investigated. When we went back to register, about
the twentieth trip, the registrar gave me this thing
to fill out again, and instead of filling it out, I wrote
down there, "It said what it meant and meant what it
said." He say, "Well, so you passed."

Winson's view of an educator:

I've never walked down the hall with a cap and gown
on, but I walked down a hall in Washington, and I
lobbied for student loans, and I lobbied for Social
Security, and I lobbied for teachers' pay raises, and
I've helped you get equal pay right here in the county,
so I'm an educator.

Winson and Dovie Hudson were committed, community
activists in rural Mississippi for decades. They, on behalf
of their children, were the first black plaintiffs to file a

school desegregation suit against the state. They were also instrumental in democratizing voter registration, establishing preschool centers, and implementing nutrition programs. With dedication and stamina, they continued to serve on boards dealing with the health, education, and welfare of their entire community.

With the assistance of Medgar Evans, Winson helped to organize the Leake County NAACP Chapter in 1960 and was its president for 38 years. She was instrumental in establishing the first Head Start Center in her community.

During my visit with Winson, she taught me the difference between "A" and "B" school lunches provided by federal funds—an A lunch included pasteurized milk in a carton; a B lunch included powdered milk. Today, in Carthage, Mississippi, you will find the Winson G. Hudson Center for children.

Jean Muirhead

Jean Muirhead had an immediate impact upon women. While serving in the Mississippi Senate in the late 1960s, she waited for an opportunity to make a difference in women's lives. The Senate faced some noncontroversial legislation that involved our juries, and Jean merely asked to insert an addendum eliminating the word *male* in the wording. Her fellow senators voted to pass the legislation, unaware of what they had done. It was the next day's newspapers that informed the senators that they opened the doors for women to serve on juries. One of the leading arguments against women serving on juries was there was only ONE bathroom in the courthouses. I shall never forget my first and only time to serve on a jury; my first impulse was to look for that bathroom. I made speeches to get women on juries, and while living in South Carolina in the early 1960s, my first television appearance was in Columbia, representing the League of Women Voters and asking for women to serve on the juries in South Carolina.

Jean was also much involved in Mississippi's International Year's program in 1977. Although Dr. Jessie Mosley was our chair, Jean was the leader at our business sessions, and that was not an easy task. The conservatives, who came and took over the business session, nominated and elected our delegates to the national convention, held in Houston, Texas, in November 1977. At the national conference, Mississippi was the only state in the Union that had two male delegates.

Left to right: Cora Norman, Governor Ray Mabus, Frances Coleman, and Pat Smith.

Frances Coleman, administrator of special collections for the Mississippi State University Library, was our voice for women at MSU. She attended all of the state-wide meetings when we pushed to have the ERA ratified and was in Jackson several times a week during the legislative session. She was very active in the Mississippi Federation of Business and Professional Women and served as president in 1991 and 1992. That organization claimed the largest number of women of any women's organization in the state, and they were always on top of issues women faced in the work place, in education, in government, and in the civic life of the state. Frances now serves as dean of libraries at MSU.

Coleman had a leading role in getting the papers of outstanding Mississippians deposited at MSU, providing students and scholars throughout the nation access to the papers of such leaders as Congressman G. V. "Sonny" Montgomery, David Bowen, Senator John C. Stennis, Hodding Carter, Norma Fields, Bill Minor, Sid Salter, Chip Pickering, John Grisham, Wiley Carter, and Turner Catledge. In her position, she worked with university administrators, faculty and students, and individuals locally, statewide, regionally, and nationally. Through civic organization responsibilities, university library collection development matters, and the Library Association, Frances established experience in working directly with state government officials, state legislators, and the Mississippi congressional delegation in Washington, D. C.

In 1981, the President's Commission on the Status of Women at Mississippi State University named Frances Coleman the Outstanding Professional Woman in Administration. In 1992, she received the Friend of Women Award from that same commission, and in 1996, the American Library Association named Frances the American Library Association Legislative and Grassroots Champion in recognition of her ongoing work with the Washington delegation.

Frances served on the Mississippi Humanities Council from 1991 through 1995. The MHC recognized her advocacy of the humanities program, her introduction of an ethnic heritage program in Starkville, her promotion of multimedia to the council, and her leadership in chairing MHC's first awards program in 1994.

Jessie Bryant Mosley worked toward a better Mississippi in many, many activities. With the opening of the first black Savings & Loan Association located on Lynch Street near Jackson State University, Jessie became its first cashier-teller because people that saw and trusted her in that position would deposit their money into the Savings and Loan. When the Mississippi Humanities Council moved from Ole Miss to Jackson, we used that Savings and Loan as our fiscal agent.

Jessie Mosley

I first met Jessie Mosley at the University of Mississippi in the mid-sixties when she was a participant in the first desegregation institute held at the University of Mississippi. Katharine Rea was involved in that institute and hosted a party for some of the participants at her home on campus; Jessie and Dorothy Height from Washington, D. C., were there.

Jessie participated in one of the early bi-racial activities when it was most risky. A small group of black and white women in Mississippi joined together and invited women from all over the nation to come quietly, and without publicity, to Mississippi to establish a network—Wednesdays in Mississippi. The women came, talked with the Mississippi women, and quietly returned to their homes. Jessie told me that these women and their churches later sent contributions when the civil rights activists came to Mississippi, ended up in jail, and then needed bail. Few people in Mississippi knew about this network, and today, in 2009, a group is gathering information to tell the story. Jessie's daughter, Wilma Clopton, is helping with that project.

For seven years, Jessie worked with the YWCA in a predominately black section of downtown Jackson. There, she took children from diverse backgrounds and instilled human dignity into them. She was able to name ministers, teachers, social workers, and other outstanding citizens throughout the nation who came through Farish Street YWCA. She recalled, after many years, the sight of a neglected toddler, the child of a local prostitute, sitting on the street curb day after day. Jessie finally took the child home with her, and he became a member of her household. He later became a minister. While her husband was in graduate school, she worked at the YWCA, and though household funds were meager, she took care of her own family of three children as well as four other girls. Through the years, Jessie and her husband sent 22 persons through four years of college; most of those graduated from Jackson State University.

In 1977, the women in Mississippi elected Jessie Mosley as chairperson of our International Women's Year meeting. We had no idea of the turmoil that would surround the statewide meeting. However, there was no one who could have handled the hostile audience of 800 anti-IWY men and women with greater success or calm than Jessie. Her sterling character carried her through the situation, and the antagonists later congratulated her for her demeanor throughout the session.

Jessie Mosley, organizer, national board member, and life member of the National Council of Negro Women in Mississippi, continued to lead that organization's activities in Mississippi. Always concerned with the welfare of children and mothers, she mounted a statewide inoculation program and a nutrition program for children. She was also concerned with the welfare of rural women who needed jobs but had no marketable skills. As director of Women in Community Service (WICS), she created a program to screen young women for Job Corps.

Jessie bolstered people, promoting their sense of personal worth as well as community values. Her spirit was infectious; her diplomacy, extraordinary; her courage, boundless. From her myriad activities and accomplishments, it was difficult to select one specific project to cite for her qualifications as a person of action. Nonetheless, her mobilization of volunteers while spearheading the Mississippi Association for the Preservation of Smith Robertson School in Jackson represented the qualities that made her unique. It was a project of lasting value for itself and of high potential for education and economic gain for the region.

Smith Robertson was the first high school for blacks in Jackson, Mississippi, and produced writer Richard Wright and many black leaders. To many, it became a symbol of pride and accomplishments within the historic black district. Yet, it closed in 1971 after the integration of schools and was to be demolished in 1977 because of decay. Then Jessie Mosley said, "We must act within our community . . . to pass on our heritage to our children." She brought disadvantaged residents of the economically depressed area and high ranking persons of means and influence together to serve on special biracial committees. They saved the school as part of the Farish Street Historical District and transformed it into the Smith Robertson Museum and Culture Center with Dr. Jessie Mosley as director. I was honored to serve for many years on their board.

In the development of the museum, Jessie had to overcome public apathy even within the black community. Many young people knew nothing of pre-civil-rights life in Mississippi or the significance of the Smith Robertson School. She also had to overcome some whites' hostility to the city's involvement in a project based on black culture. The major obstacle, however, was economic, since the drive for funds coincided with a major recession and high unemployment.

One morning I received a telephone call from one of the museum's staff members, who requested I, as a board member, attend the budget meeting at City Hall that night in support of Jessie's request for funding. I discovered that the city allocated $150,000 of federal funds to the Smith Robertson Museum and Culture Center. When Jessie got up to defend the receipt of those funds, she said, "Forget the $150,000; I need $300,000." John Peoples, president of Jackson State University and another board member, turned to me and asked, "What is Jessie planning to use these funds for?" Jessie made her case, and although they denied her request for $300,000, she received more than the $150,000 first budgeted.

At last, renovations started on the inside of the building. While work continued, Dr. Mosley secured from the Smithsonian in Washington, D. C., their traveling exhibit "From Field to Factory," showing the migration of blacks from Mississippi. The opening of that exhibit would claim members of the Smithsonian board, so Dr. Mosley planned a reception in the soon-to-be renovated building. Just weeks before the opening, the museum was still a mess, and the carpenters informed Dr. Mosley that the renovations could not be completed as scheduled. She replied, "Then get your tools, and get out of my way!" As it turned out, they completed the work, cleaned up the museum, and held the reception as scheduled for the opening of the exhibit.

The first Folklife Festival held at the Smith Robertson Museum and Cultural Center was memorable. Dr. Corrine Anderson and I had the job of making homemade ice cream! Because of the demand for it, we literally tore the bottom from her grandmother's ice cream freezer!

Jessie Mosley served on the Mississippi Humanities Council as an appointee of Governor William Winter from 1981 to 1984 and was on the planning committee for the Tenth Anniversary Conference. In 1994, she again joined the council as an appointee of Governor Kirk Fordice, but she resigned in 1996. Her resolution presented when she ended her tenure in 1984:

> Jessie Mosley, attending "Time Has Come" in Greenville, was the belle of the Blues Cruise; she led the dancing and charmed the owner of a private yacht for a private tour of the river. She hosted Carole Watson from NEH on a whirlwind tour of North Mississippi, including a tour of Elvis Presley's home which was a MUST for Carole Watson.

During the last years of my tenure with the MHC, Jessie was by my side supporting me. We made many trips together, and after my retirement, we went regularly to the boat in Vicksburg to gamble. On our last drive, she directed me to a place in Jackson where she wanted to place a conference center to deal with many problems but especially to teach young people manners. When Jessie was dying, I visited her. Her son Gene, forever by her side during those last days, asked me to help get her out of bed and into a wheelchair. I was unable to hold her, and she fell to the floor. She smiled at me and said, "Cora, I'm all right!" What a woman!

Jessie Mosley visited three presidents at the White House. President Nixon invited her with a task force on hunger; she presented the IWY Plan of Action to President Carter, and she represented the National Council of Negro Women at a meeting with President Reagan. Along with Jessie Jackson, she received the national Religious Heritage of America award for contributions to her community. In 1997, the Hinds County Department of Human Services named their building in her honor—the Dr. Jessie B. Mosley Building.

Left to right: Cora Norman and
Jessie Mosley at the White House.

Katharine Rea in Alaska.

Katharine Rea was a member of the Mississippi Humanities Council from 1984 to 1988 and in 1996 received the Public Humanities Achievement Award from the council. It was hard for me to sit down and write about the woman who was not only my teacher, but my counselor, my companion on numerous trips—Alaska, Mexico, England, Scotland, and Ireland—and my role model. I am so indebted to her for the opportunity she gave me by recommending me for the job of executive director of the Mississippi Humanities Council. She never disclosed that fact to me until after my retirement. However, I knew she was always there with encouragement and advice, and I should have involved her from the very first because of her knowledge of literature and her commitment to the disciplines of the humanities. However, in those early years we never recognized a professor in the schools of education as being a humanities scholar. However, she certainly promoted the public humanities program.

Katharine had such an impact upon my life, almost from the moment we arrived in Oxford, Mississippi. I met her at an AAUW meeting, and she supported my application for an AAUW scholarship that helped me through a master's degree program at the University of Mississippi. I no sooner received that degree than Katharine suggested that I might like to take some additional graduate courses, eventually leading to my Ph.D.

Women's Studies is now an accepted academic course, but Katharine offered the first women's course at the University of Mississippi years before the course became so well known. Her students, men as well as women, referred to it as they talked about the issues unveiled in the course—"Have you had the 'Course'?" She had an interest in all her students. Some said that she took the uneducated and educated them, the unlovely and made them acceptable, the meek and instilled into them assertiveness, the belligerent and tamed them. Her parties were numerous and remembered by all. Katharine highlighted any student attainment with a party at her home. I attended more celebrations at her house on Sorority Row than any other place, and I'm confident that many of her students would attest to her hospitality there.

Dr. Rea was the first counselor in the Gulfport High School, dean of women at Ole Miss, and later professor of higher education in their School of Education. Her work with the Mississippi Association of Women's Deans and Counselors was legendary. She was the DEAN of deans. She worked on their program committees to ensure that all deans and counselors were on top of the issues and concerns in their professions. She worked tirelessly for legislation for Title IX and Affirmative Action which, without the Equal Rights Amendment, is slowly but steadily eroding.

While Katharine was dean of women at Ole Miss, James Meredith enrolled there. As the institution sought to keep the status quo, Dean Rea was almost a solitary figure in trying to prepare students and faculty to accept change in their lives. She offered sensitivity workshops for selected leaders that we might examine our inner feelings and question, for the first time for many of us, why we sustained a society that took away human dignity from all black citizens. She was unwavering in her resolute support of equality of opportunity for all peoples. She was one of the very first white educators to work for the merger of the two professional educational associations in Mississippi. For several years she sacrificed her personal weekends to drive from Oxford to Jackson to be "the" white as the Mississippi Teachers Association worked through the details of the merger.

A Methodist church in Memphis, Tennessee, hosted the first biracial event I ever attended. They invited two adults, one black and one white, and two young people, one black and one white, from selected communities, including Oxford, Mississippi, for a five-day meeting. My first thoughts were that the room probably had only one bed and I would be expected to sleep with my black friend. What would my daddy say? I went to Katharine. She simply suggested that I get a private room, but there was no money for one. What a relief I felt when I went into the room and found two beds. However, I must confess that after two days, I called my husband to come and pick me up. We drove back to Memphis on Friday to pick up the other three individuals from Oxford. All the way back to Oxford, my black friend Della Davidson said to me, "Some just do not have the strength for their convictions." How right she was!

Upon her retirement from the University of Mississippi, where she was a woman to be reckoned with for 26 years, Dr. Rea was cited as follows:

> For her selfless investment of time and concern for the progress of her scores of doctoral students [of whom I was one]; for her admirable humanitarian interests and resolute support of equality of opportunity for all peoples; and for her keen interest and effort on behalf of improving the status of women.

Dr. Rea helped women to experience a liberal education. She worked to elevate human beings—be they professional, graduate or undergraduate students, housewives, or housemothers.

Dr. Rea paved the way for the mature woman to experience higher education by going out of her way to make them more comfortable and to help in any way possible wherever the need. I remembered going with her to the Gulf Coast to ensure a mature woman would go to summer school at Ole Miss. We drove behind that woman all the way back to Oxford to assure her that she was not going to Oxford by herself. Dr. Rea developed educational programs at the University of Mississippi for rural women. She early recognized the need for women on policy making boards if we were to improve the status of women.

Clarice Campbell, *sitting*; and Katharine Rea.

Over 60 people, of whom 40 were women, received doctoral degrees because of her care and concern—which never ceased at graduation but seemed to be a life-long commitment on her part to continue to write letters of recommendation as needed for promotion in one's professional life.

Upon her retirement from the University of Mississippi, Katharine moved immediately to the Gulf Coast and continued her involvement with civic groups. She was a recognized leader in AAUW, and the Endowed Fund for Research and Projects bears her name. She actively served the League of Women Voters as its president, served on the state boards of the Mississippi Association for Mental Health and the Mississippi Council on Human Relations, and was active on the Gulf Coast with book clubs, the Rape Crisis Center, and the Gulf Coast Symphony and Opera. She was also the official fund raiser for all worthy community projects. She was, indeed, the scholar who thought privately and spoke and acted publicly.

Left to right: Imogene Borganelli and Katharine Rea.

In the 1990s, Imogene Borganelli, Katharine Rea, and I planned a trip to the United Kingdom. After Imogene and I purchased our tickets to Manchester, England, we discovered that Katharine would not go with us but would arrive two days later in London. Katharine was committed to an opera fund raiser on the Gulf Coast—she never changed her commitments. Imogene and I got to Manchester, rented a car, and left the airport only to find that neither of us knew how to shift into reverse gear. We drove for blocks, and finally Imogene got out to direct traffic while I turned the car around without using the reverse gear. We stopped at the first gas station, and Imogene rushed to a car parked at one of the gas pumps and asked if they knew how we could get our car into reverse. It was so simple—just press down on the top of the gearshift!

The next morning, we knew we had to get to London that day in order to meet Katharine when she arrived. It was snowing so hard that we could not read the road signs. We stopped more than once so Imogene could get out of the car to wipe the snow off the road sign so we would know which direction to go. The motorway around London must be 200 miles long, and we took the wrong direction to get to Gatwick Airport.

We wanted to stay at a B & B near the airport in order to arrive at the airport before Katharine did. That evening, after checking into a B & B, we asked where to go for dinner. They directed us to a restaurant not too far away to walk, but we had to walk through a cemetery. We took off, and when we got to the cemetery we found there were no lights. We grabbed each other, and I can still feel the relief we felt when we finally saw the lights of the restaurant. Katharine arrived the next morning and was ready to travel. What a wonderful trip we had in England and Scotland, returning to London for our flight home.

Standing left to right: Jewel Garner, Wes Cady, and Norma Fields. *Seated left to right:* Cora Norman and Katharine Rea.

Left to right: Elise and Governor William Winter, and Katharine Rea.

Dr. Rea will long be remembered as an educator and as a social activist, but her record for equality of opportunity in Mississippi's turbulent 60s was unmatched by any other woman in the state. Hers was a voice of reason at the most traditional of all institutions. She was a friend to so many, a mentor to many, and one who dared to enter into the arena of life and fight for that which she thought was right, just, and fair. She was one of the most recognized agents of change in Mississippi during the twentieth century.

Katharine was my role model as a professional woman. But, we traveled after her retirement, creating many memories for me. We went to Northern Ireland in 1993, at a time when there was much unrest in Belfast. When we rented a car at the Shannon Airport, they told me not to take the car into Northern Ireland. We headed South and toured the southern coast. We stayed at B & B's and each morning around the breakfast table answered the question of where we were going. Katharine always replied, "And, we're going to Belfast." I had no plans to go to Belfast. However, after two or three days in Dublin, I decided that if Katharine wanted to go to Belfast so badly I would go with her.

Left to right: Cora Norman and Katharine
Rea. New Year's Day, Dublin, Ireland.

We left the car in Dublin and took the train to Belfast. When we got to Belfast and into a taxi, heavily armed British soldiers stopped us at each intersection and asked, "Where are you going?" We stayed one night at a B & B and returned to Dublin the next day. When we got into the taxi before lunch that morning and asked the driver to take us to the depot for a 3 p.m. train to Dublin, the driver said, "I cannot leave you ladies at the depot for such a long wait. Let me take you to a hotel where you can have lunch, and you can get a taxi from there nearer the time you are to catch your train." We agreed. When we got to the hotel, we found it was behind a barricade; the doors of the hotel were locked; a tank was outside the barricade, and soldiers were everywhere. It was an experience, and one that I would not have had without Katharine's determination to see it all. Today, I am grateful for it.

Katharine Rea in Belfast, Ireland.

Our last trip together was to New York to celebrate her birthday. The highlight of that trip for her was lunch at the Tavern on the Green with a former student, George Abraham, whom she admired so much. At that time, she was unable to walk around the block, so we hailed taxis and continued to go. What a woman!

Katharine Rea

Left to right: Cora Norman and Katharine Rea.

Left to right: Katharine Rea, Boyd Golding, and Cora Norman.

My Early Retirement Years

For years I worked with Dr. Ally Mack, head of international relations at Jackson State University, and after I retired, I dearly wanted to travel internationally to learn more about the different cultures in our world. Gemma Beckley continues to travel extensively, taking numerous groups of Fulbright-Hays scholars abroad, and I am deeply indebted to her for much of my international travel since retirement.

Immediately upon my retirement from the Mississippi Humanities Council in 1996, Gemma included me in a group of scholars going to China for six weeks with a grant from the Fulbright-Hays program to observe the status of women. In 2004, she included me with another group of Fulbright-Hays scholars going to South Africa for six weeks to again look at the changing status of women.

The following year, 2005, I went with Gemma to southern India to attend an international conference on women at Marian College, where she was the keynote speaker. I never had an international trip like that one. She was the dignitary, but the college treated me as such, even though I was merely along to carry her bags. V. T. Samuel, chair of the social work department at the college, met us at the airport in Cochi and drove us to the campus. Upon arrival at the college, the president and key officials met us and presented a rose to each of us. Although designed for social workers—and again I felt out of my academic route—it was truly a humanities conference. Afterward, Dr. Samuel and his wife took us on a three-day sightseeing trip before returning us to the Cochi airport for departure.

Shortly after returning from India, I spent 10 days in Scotland with Bill and Judy and Phil. It was an interesting trip with much personalized attention from airport security thanks to Bill's artificial hip and numerous pubs.

In 2006, Judy and I returned to England for a week; I was able to visit Clovelly and Dover once again.

Gemma's husband David Beckley, president of Rust College, was responsible for naming me to their board of trustees after I retired. I served as chairman of the academic committee for several years, and it was an honor to be elected an emeritus member of the board at the end of my term. David allowed me to represent Rust College as a Fulbright-Hays scholar in South Africa, for which I was very grateful. Visiting colleges and universities broadened my international relations and gave me valuable and memorable experiences.

By 2007, Gemma Beckley received more Fulbright-Hays grants to take scholars abroad than any other person. Not only a highly productive scholar in social work, she changed the former perception that a college president's wife should simply welcome visitors to the college with a cup of tea. The *Mississippi Journal* honored her in 2008 as one of the 50 Top Business Women in Mississippi.

Dr. David Beckley, president of Rust College, joined the MHC after I retired, but he was always an ardent supporter of our work. Because of him, we had a close working relationship with Rust College and its' humanities faculty.

David and Gemma Beckley

David became president of Rust College in 1993 and is now (2009) the longest tenured senior college president in Mississippi. When the college last prepared for its accreditation renewal with the Southern Regional Association of Colleges and Universities, I was present when an outside panel met with members of the faculty. I was amazed that David furnished additional details to every response his faculty members made to questions posed by the visitors. It was evident that he was very much aware of everything on the Rust College campus. He honored me recently by sending an email and signing it "Your adopted son."

In the years following my retirement, Leslie McLemore gave me much credit in the public domain for bringing races together to talk about issues. In 2007, it was Les who got Jackson 2000 to recognize me, along with former Jackson Mayor Harvey Johnson, at their annual Friendship Ball. Harvey and I led the dancers to the floor that night. I never learned to dance because I was raised a Baptist; my mother told me it was sinful. I learned later that my mother was quite a dancer in her younger days, and at the 2007 Friendship Ball, after four glasses of Scotch, I took to the dance floor and had a wonderful evening. All of which I owe to Leslie McLemore.

In 2007, Bill and I moved to Crossville, Tennessee, and in 2008, Judy and Phil and I spent two weeks in Ireland. I'm ready for another trip!

2009 began with the exciting announcement that I was one of six recipients of the 2009 Fannie Lou Hamer Humanitarian Award. It was presented in Jackson in April, and I am honored to be one of very few whites to receive the award.

Leslie Burl McLemore was responsible for the following Resolution presented to me by the Mississippi Humanities Council.

---

for
Dr. Cora Norman

Whereas Dr. Cora Norman has served with distinction as Executive Director of the Mississippi Humanities Council for twenty-four years, 1972-1996, the first and only director the Council has ever had; and

Whereas Dr. Norman created, gave form and structure and purpose and organization and life itself to an entity that did not previously exist; and

Whereas the Mississippi Committee for the Humanities and later Mississippi Humanities Council under her direction has achieved a reputation for bringing scholars in the humanities and ordinary citizens of Mississippi into dialogue beneficial and educational for both groups; and

Whereas her concern for reaching all citizens of the state and for making their voices heard, especially voices of women, African Americans, Native Americans, and other minorities, has made MHC the vehicle for building coalitions among such groups, often where no possibility of coalition existed before; and

Whereas Dr. Norman has worked regionally and nationally as a pioneer in making the humanities available and important to the public, serving on committees and as advisor to the National Endowment for the Humanities, working to found the Federation of State Humanities Councils, urging regional collaborations that have led to such ongoing projects as the Southern Humanities Media Fund, and has won numerous awards and commendations for her achievements; and

Whereas her tireless efforts, extraordinary energy, and dynamic skills in working with a variety of publics have brought the MHC to prominence in the state and brought Mississippi to national attention in positive ways through numerous Charles Frankel Awards in the Humanities, Mississippi members of the Federation Board of Directors, bringing powerful Congressional leaders from this state to publicly indicate their staunch support of funding for the humanities, and in numerous other ways, great and small;

Therefore the Mississippi Humanities Council resolves to bid Dr. Cora Norman farewell on this occasion, wishing her the best of good fortune as she moves on to exciting new adventures and bolder challenges, while at the same time relying on her continuing interest and support for an organization that owes her a tremendous debt of gratitude, for all that the Council is, it has become through her efforts.

A long-time friend, Norma Fields, wrote the following newspaper article when she heard of my retirement.

MARCH 18, 1996   MISSISSIPPI BUSINESS JOURNAL

California Dreamin'

A salute to Dr. Cora Norman

By Norma Fields

She has worked tirelessly throughout Mississippi for 25 years in an unstinting effort to forge understanding and tolerance among the different races and cultures.

These largely unsung efforts have spanned communities from academe to the ghetto, from posh suburbs to red clay hills, Delta farms and Coastal waterfronts, from the state Capitol to the nation's Capitol, and all points in between.

Through it all, she has maintained an equilibrium of her very own, going flawlessly groomed from one place to another, unflappable, speaking softly but firmly and, most important, listening closely and with good humor to whomever it is she is currently dealing with.

Her name is Cora Norman, a woman with a Ph.D. in education administration who has been the executive director of Mississippi Humanities Council since 1972 but who, unfortunately for Mississippi, is retiring later this year.

You no doubt read elsewhere of the often-brave exploits and undertakings of the Humanities Council under Dr. Norman's leadership; the times when whites wouldn't meet with blacks and there weren't many places to hold public meetings; the successes when cultures did finally meet and learn together.

Here, however, you will read about Cora Norman my friend, a sort of "I Remember Cora."

I am proud to call her my friend. In that role she has been a marvelous traveling companion (she is well-groomed, with every blonde hair in place even in her pajamas!), a sympathetic listener when I've been down, a cheerful supporter when I've been up, a fierce competitor at the bridge table, and an inspiration in how to deal with people with whom you don't necessarily agree.

With her unfailing good humor, she subtly tried, but unfortunately failed, to teach me how to be a feminist without being obnoxious. It has to be one of her very few failures, and it is my fault, not hers.

I first met Cora Norman in 1973 when I was invited to speak at a joint meeting of the Oxford League of Women Voters and the AAUW. I was taking radiation for cancer at the time, so I did not suffer fools gladly. During the question/answer period after my talk, a pesky, ultra rightwinger kept bugging me with inane political statements disguised as questions. Just as I was about to leap over the podium and throttle that babe, Cora Norman rescued the entire meeting – and me – with a very astute question that put the session back on track.

Our paths would cross numerous times, but we became friends after we were coincidentally transferred to Jackson in our separate jobs 20 years ago. It was a Cora's condo that you could meet some of the most interesting and successful people in public and private life and I especially remember meeting there Dr. Jesse Mosley, who had a lot of help from the Humanities Council and Cora Norman personally in establishing the Smith Robertson Museum in Jackson, now a widely respected repository of the history and accomplishments of Americans of African ancestry.

Then there was Judge Lucy Howorth, a couple of revolutionist women from the Philippines, who told us how things were going under the new leadership of Corazon Aquino; a young woman Sen. John C. Stennis had sent to find out "what the women of Mississippi want." And if that young woman took everything back to Stennis that the women in Cora's condo told her that night, she had a load to carry.

Another time, some of us got into a whale of an argument with a couple of Republican good ole boys from Louisiana who had brought their wives to Cora's condo for a post-game part when Ole Miss played LSU. They were the best-natured Republicans I ever met.

But Cora is not just all of these things, she is more — including a wonderful daughter whose elderly ailing mother now lives with her in that small condo; and she is a marvelous mother who is in frequent touch with her two adult children and their children.

As one of the most interesting and unique of women, I shall always remember Cora Norman and all of the kind, thoughtful things she did for me before I moved to California.

But, most of all, I shall remember Cora, impeccably groomed as always, climbing a steep, wet, slippery path in Clovelly, a tiny village on the Atlantic Coast of England, while wearing high heeled boots!

What a woman!

Norma Fields, an award winning journalist is a transplanted Mississippian whose column appears occasionally in the Mississippi Business Journal.

I was touched when I read the following note from Aurelia
Young, who was so involved in our early programs.

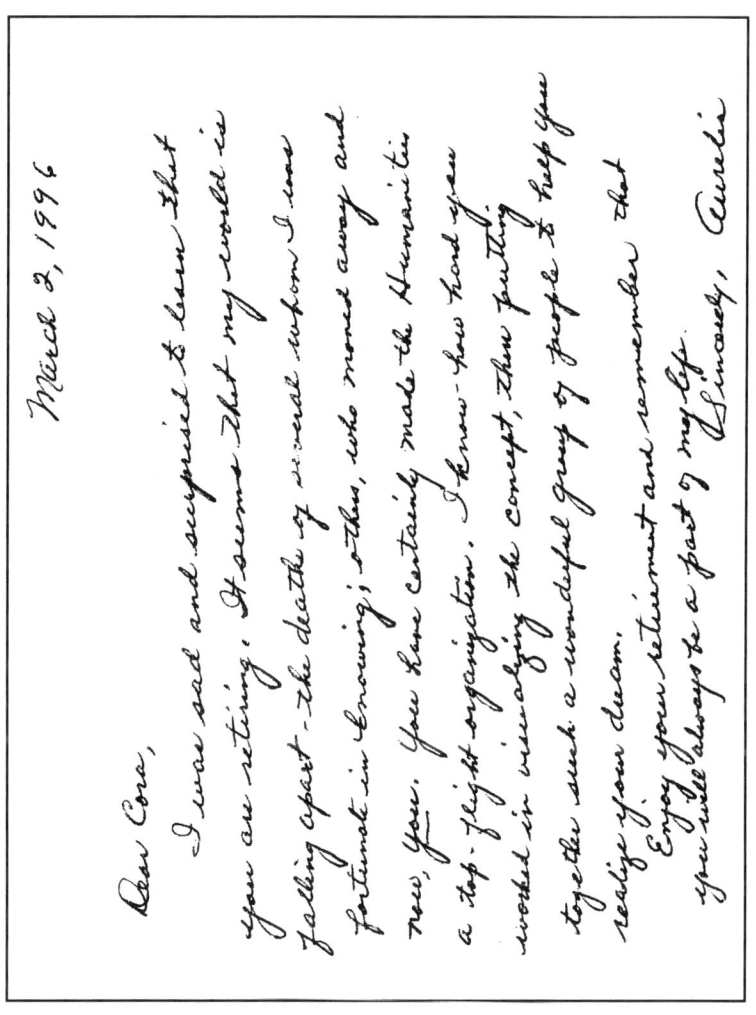

Marjorie Berlincourt, long-time staff member at NEH, wrote the following letter.

Marjorie Berlincourt

May 12, 1996

Dr. Cora Norman
Executive Director
Mississippi Humanities Council
3825 Ridgewood Road, Room 311
Jackson, MS 39211-6463

Dear Cora,

Yesterday I received a copy of the Spring 1996 newsletter of the Mississippi Humanities Council, announcing your retirement from MHC. For 24 years your service to the humanities in Mississippi and nationwide has been invaluable. The programs you initiated have stimulated discussion of the issues of major importance for the people of your state. During the seven years I served as director of the Division of State Programs at the National Endowment for the Humanities, I looked forward with the greatest pleasure to our meetings. Yours was always the voice of reason and good humor in the midst of sometimes rancorous discussions between the various state directors and the national staff.

You should be very proud of the major contributions you have made to your state through your leadership of MHC. Through your unstinting efforts you have created goodwill and have increased respect for the importance of the humanities in the lives of everyone. All of us who have worked with you over the years know that the next phase of your life will be equally fulfilling.

With my very best wishes and my congratulations on a most distinguished career,

Cordially,

Marjorie A. Berlincourt

7844 Langley Ridge Road   McLean, Virginia 22102   (703) 893-7672

My friend, Elbert R. Hilliard, not only wrote a letter but included a Resolution from the Mississippi Historical Society.

MISSISSIPPI HISTORICAL SOCIETY
P. O. Box 571
JACKSON, MISSISSIPPI 39205

May 17, 1996

Dr. Cora Norman
Executive Director
Mississippi Humanities Council
3825 Ridgewood Road, Room 311
Jackson, Mississippi 39211-6463

Dear Cora:

I am enclosing a resolution that was adopted by the Board of Directors of the Mississippi Historical Society at the Board's meeting on May 4, 1996, to commend you for your outstanding contributions to educational progress and the preservation of our state's cultural heritage and to express appreciation for your longstanding support of the Society and the Department of Archives and History. I am indebted to Katie Blount for her splendid work in drafting the resolution.

You have left your mark on the state through your work with the Mississippi Humanities Council, and we want you to know that we have enjoyed working with you. You have set a standard for service and performance that could well be emulated by every public official.

We shall look forward to our continued association and hope that, although you are retiring as Executive Director of the Humanities Council, you will stay involved in the work of the Mississippi Historical Society.

With every good wish and appreciation of your support and interest, I am

Sincerely,

Elbert R. Hilliard
Secretary-Treasurer

ERH:cs
Enclosure

RESOLUTION OF COMMENDATION

WHEREAS, Dr. Cora Norman has announced her retirement as executive director of the Mississippi Humanities Council; and

WHEREAS, Dr. Norman has guided the Humanities Council with great energy and distinction since 1972; and

WHEREAS, under Dr. Norman's leadership, the Mississippi Humanities Council has demonstrated an outstanding commitment to promoting the study of history, literature, language, and philosophy in Mississippi; and

WHEREAS, by channeling grant money from the National Endowment for the Humanities to cultural and educational organizations around Mississippi, the Humanities Council has made tremendous progress in increasing the general public's appreciation of the humanities; and

WHEREAS, the Mississippi Department of Archives and History is especially indebted to Dr. Norman and the Humanities Council for their generous help in establishing the Scholar-in-Residence Program, through which the Department has brought scholars to the Archives to catalogue, translate, and annotate manuscripts in the collection; and

WHEREAS, one of the Humanities Council's most recent contributions to the preservation and interpretation of Mississippi's heritage—a preliminary survey of oral history holdings around the state—will serve as an invaluable resource for students of Mississippi history and culture; and

WHEREAS, Dr. Norman's contributions to the cultural life of Mississippi extend beyond her leadership of the Humanities Council to include service on the national board and as state president of the American Association of University Women and as a member of the Mississippi State Advisory Commission to the U.S. Commission on Civil Rights;

NOW, THEREFORE, BE IT RESOLVED by the Board of Directors of the Mississippi Historical Society, assembled in Jackson, Mississippi, on May 4, 1996, that Dr. Cora Norman be commended for her outstanding contributions to educational progress and cultural vitality in Mississippi, and for her long-standing support of the Mississippi Historical Society;

BE IT FURTHER RESOLVED that Dr. Norman be sent a copy of this resolution.

Elbert R. Hilliard
Secretary-Treasurer

Samuel B. Olden
President

My friend, Leslie R. Myers, Arts Columnist for the Clarion Ledger, wrote a very complimentary article upon my retirement.

LESLIE R. MYERS

Arts Columnist
The Clarion-Ledger

Norman retires from job, but not from active life

Cora Norman is retired. But the light has not gone out.

Like recruiting moths to a flame, Norman has encouraged — no, made — Mississippians talk about tough or timely issues for 24 years.

Forums from the fine arts to racial angst to Southern politics have materialized, thanks to the Mississippi Humanities Council.

Since 1972, the council and Cora Norman have been synonymous. She was a co-founder of the statewide agency and its only executive director, until this summer.

"It has been the best job one can imagine — and I had it," Norman, of Jackson, said. "I don't think there have been any low points."

Norman wouldn't have noticed them. She is known for being inspired, driven and optimistically relentless. She leaves the $53,500 job with a sense of accomplishment. "It has given me a vehicle to bring different cultures together to discuss in a civil way, with civility — instead of shooting each other, fighting each other, cussing each other or not even talking to each other. And that's been my bag. People are my bag."

Norman

No sunsets in sight

Norman, 69, stepped down May 31. Her successor is Barbara Carpenter, who was assistant executive director for a decade. The agency is administered by a 22-member council.

Norman's "retirement" lasted only three weeks. She just received a Fulbright-Hayes Scholarship. She will fly to China on Tuesday to attend a five-week women's studies seminar. Her personal focus is women in politics.

"My interest always has been women and issues that women face," the Columbia County, Ark., native said. When she returns from China, she plans to re-establish a statewide women's network, which was most active in the early 1980s.

Her other pet project has been another civil rights issue. As head of the council, she is most proud of "the involvement of black leadership in Mississippi — not only as council members and (council) chairs, but as project directors throughout the state."

Norman also helped launch the 13-state Southern Humanities Council coalition and the Federation of State Humanities Councils, a national lobbying group.

At the Federation's May 2 meeting in Washington, both Mississippi senators, Thad Cochran and Trent Lott, expressed enthusiasm and support for humanities councils, particularly Mississippi's, Norman noted.

The Mississippi Humanities Council is funded by the National Endowment for the Humanities and private donations. (The Mississippi Legislature has given nothing.)

Like all cultural agencies, the NEH is on the U.S. Congress' budget chopping block (or guillotine). But Norman thinks the national endowment and, thus, the Mississippi Humanities Council, will survive "if citizens will write enough letters" to Congress.

That is, like Norman, never say never.

I received a letter from T. W. Lewis, who was very involved
with the Mississippi Humanities Council's activities.

MILLSAPS COLLEGE

July 16, 1996

Dr. Cora Norman
5025 Wayneland Dr., #G-1
Jackson Ms 39211

Dear Cora:

It seems as if our schedules and the demands upon
us have kept us from making contact this spring
and summer, but I did not want another day to pass
without writing to you, even though right now you
are probably soaking up culture in China. My
retirement, bringing matters at the College to
closure, and to say nothing of moving out of an
office I have occupied for 32 years, pretty well
absorbed me. Then Julia had emergency surgery
(she's okay now, but it was scary until they found
out it was her gall bladder), and we have been to
Chicago for a visit with our son Tom. All of this
is to say that I have been distracted with
conflicts from properly congratulating you on your
sterling career at MHC and expressing my own deep
appreciation not only for the signal contributions
you have made to the state, the Federation, and to
NEH, but also for the good friendship I have
enjoyed with you now for over twelve years.

You have taken and sent others with the treasures
of the humanities to virtually every nook and
cranny of the state. You have given humanities
scholars the opportunity to develop further their
own expertise and share that with persons outside
of the academy. And you have brought together
persons of diverse backgrounds and beliefs to
share common commitments. You have made the good
witness for justice in matters of race, gender and
class. And you have done this with a grace and
charm that amazes me. I have also observed how
your work has energized you, and how your
enthusiasm for it has been infectious for those of
us who were privileged to serve with you. So now
that you and I have "quit our day jobs," Julia and
I wish you all of the rewards that can come with
the satisfaction of work well done..

We are taking your cue that travel is a great way
to celebrate one's retirement. We leave on July
24 for Munich, Salzburg, Vienna, and Prague. And
we are as excited about this as we can be. We
hope that your trip is rich with all the treasures
that you anticipated.

Best,

J. W.

1701 NORTH STATE ST.

JACKSON · MS · 39210

(601) 974-1000

I received another letter of congratulations from Constance Slaughter-Harvey.

Constance Iona Slaughter-Harvey
ATTORNEY AT LAW

POST OFFICE BOX 88
FOREST, MISSISSIPPI 39074
601-469-4210 (H)

SIX CEES LAW BUILDING - SUITE A
516 JONES STREET
601-469-0990

July 17, 1996

Dr. Cora Norman
Mississippi Humanities Council
Jackson, Mississippi

Dear Cora:

I feel quite guilty when I ask you to overlook my delinquency regarding your retirement. Perhaps I delayed because I did not want to accept your departure. On the other hand, I probably accepted it (even though I did not want to) but refused to acknowledge it. Nevertheless I will miss you very much. The state will miss you very much (even though the majority of the citizens will not realize that we are heading in a backward position) and I will personally feel rather odd knowing that you are not at the helm of the Humanities boat. There is no telling where we are going and how we will get there. How do you intend to spend your free time? Any plans to travel the world?

Please continue to stay in touch because I respect and admire persons who have help others in a less fortunate status. This is what your entire professional life has been about and will continue to be about. You are special because you have that commitment ... we are where we are (in a good sense) because you sacrificed much for us. Thanks!

Let me know if you are ever in the Forest area and we'll do lunch as made/prepared/cooked by my sister who is an excellent after hours cook.

Thanks for your generous expression of congratulations to Constance. She is now in the business of 'floating loans' to those of us who need financial relief and she has already set a limit.

Thanks for caring and thanks for sharing.

Sincerely yours,

Connie

Constance Slaughter-Harvey

/ci

I was delighted to receive a letter from my very dear friend,
Robert Smith, M. D.

CENTRAL MISSISSIPPI HEALTH SERVICES, INC.

1134 Winter Street
JACKSON,MISSISSIPPI 39204

(601)948-5572
FAX (601)353-7070

July 17, 1996

Dr. Cora Norman
Executive Director
MS Humanities Council
3825 Ridgewood Road, Room 311
Jackson, MS 39211-6453

Dear Dr. Norman:

I salute you for being the founding Executive Director of
the Mississippi Humanities Council and for heading that agency
for the past 24 years. You have certainly left the state a
better place.

Our state needed the Council and you as its director in 1982
when we were trying to come out of the throes of civil rights and
so many issues that lacked humanity. It has been through your
leadership, your counsel, and the enormous energy and drive that
you have brought people and projects together that would have
been unthinkable without someone who was bold, creative, and yet
understood how the humanities interact in our lives.

I trust that you will enjoy a great trip to China. I will
always be grateful to you for the support that you have given to
activities and programs all over the state and especially those
in which I have had an opportunity to work with you.

I am,

Very sincerely yours,

Robert Smith, M.D.
Director

RS/rml

Robert Cheatham presented a "Tribute to Cora Norman" on behalf of the Federation of State Humanities Councils.

FEDERATION OF
STATE HUMANITIES
COUNCILS

1600 Wilson Boulevard
Suite 902
Arlington, Virginia 22209

703/908-9700 telephone
703/908-9706 fax

Tribute to Cora Norman

I've been asked to say a few words about Cora Norman. As you all know if you were at "Humanities on the Hill," we've done this, so it's the Craig Eisendrath Memorial Tribute. So I'll be brief.

Upon retirement most state humanities council directors deserve a memorial, an acknowledgement of our indebtedness for their past accomplishments. Cora Norman deserves a monument, a permanent public reminder that she continues to lead the way to where we should be. Under Cora's leadership, the Mississippi Humanities Council routinely demonstrated that everyone in Congress is reachable, that they can all be made to understand and publicly support our work. Even more importantly, the Mississippi Humanities Council under Cora's leadership served as a model for all of us who believe that the work of the state councils can heal our nation's racial divisions. Cora accomplished this exemplary work with all the charm and grace that the South is known for and with her own brand of determination. The work of the state councils is eternally in her debt. Thank you.

Presented by Robert Cheatham
On behalf of the Federation of State Humanities Councils
September 8, 1996

A letter which I certainly treasured from Jamil Zainaldin, president of the Federation of State Humanities Councils follows.

 FEDERATION OF
STATE HUMANITIES
COUNCILS

1600 Wilson Boulevard
Suite 902
Arlington, Virginia 22209

703/908-9700 telephone
703/908-9706 fax

December 2, 1996

Dear Cora,

We at the Federation would very much like to be with you at this event in your honor, but please know that we are with you in spirit, and we send you all our best wishes and warmest gratitude for the many gifts you have given to the Federation and the public humanities during your long and distinguished career with the Mississippi Humanities Council.

Among your many contributions--and our many debts--is your unflagging leadership in the area of advocacy. You have taught all of us how to make the case for the humanities with Congress, and the effectiveness with which you made that case over and over to your own Mississippi delegation has reaped benefits for all the state councils. The "Cora Norman" style and talent in this area cannot be matched, but you have provided us a standard that we will strive to live up to.

We are also grateful for the many ways you have helped to define the state humanities councils as a vital movement. The outstanding leaders from Mississippi, such as your current chair, Leslie McLemore, who have served on the Federation board over the years have helped immeasurably in moving the Federation forward to meet the challenges of a constantly changing climate and a steadily evolving membership.

Finally, we are both humbled and inspired by the quiet bridge-building you have done in Mississippi and among the state councils. Your tireless efforts to bring together people of different races in Mississippi and to encourage civil discourse in all arenas, from programmatic to political to personal, are a shining example of what the public humanities should be all about.

Maggi, Esther and I salute you, and we send you our deepest respect and affection.

Sincerely,

Jamil Zainaldin
President

My letter of thanks to the members of the Mississippi Humanities Council for the reception they hosted in my honor December 5, 1996.

ᛁnternational Cultural Exchange
CORA NORMAN, Ph.D.

5 December 1996

Members of the
Mississippi Humanities Council
3825 Ridgewood Road
Jackson, MS 39211

Dear Friends:

       I can not adequately express my gratitude for the extravaganza you staged in my behalf last Tuesday night. It was a wonderful night for Cora! Surely that was the best send-off you could have given to me to launch my retirement. The presence of so many of the people who had been involved from the beginning of the state humanities program and so many who have been involved in recent years certainly attest to the strength of the program today. The respect the agency has gained through the years is due to the work of so many staunch citizens--not just Cora. We can all share in the pride of the respect the Council claims in the state today.

       The charter membership of the Council included eighteen of Mississippi's most prominent citizens. I used their names to open doors for me in communities throughout the state. The membership through the years has continued to attract those citizens of note and the present Council is no exception. It has indeed been a privilege to work for such people. I was most fortunate to have been offered the job and given the opportunity by Porter Fortune, John Bettersworth, Estus Smith, Tom Flynn and Parham Williams to mount a public humanities program for Mississippi. The job never ceased to be most challenging and rewarding.

5025 Wayneland Drive • Apartment G-1 • Jackson, MS 39211 • U.S.A. • (601) 956-7107

We can all share in the diversity of MHC's friends as was evidenced at the Awards Banquet. That is my greatest pleasure. When the Council was organized in 1972 few organizations claimed both blacks and whites not even our churches. The initial group came together "eyeing" each other, bringing much baggage of distrust, but they were good people and out of their doubts and even bad past experiences grew mutual respect for each other. Some had to bite their biases but were willing to do so for the common good. We owe that group recognition for their tolerance, their good will and for their determination to create a better Mississippi.

The present Council members have an enviable legacy in the annals of the state-based humanities program nationwide. I have no doubt that with the current leadership the in-put to the national program as well as in Mississippi will be just as noteworthy as its past history. With Jack White as the new Chair, Gemma Beckley the Vice Chair, and the list of notables as members you will set your goals broad. Just don't forget the small rural communities in this state! (I just can't help giving advice, can I? It's in my blood!)

I must add one more admonition: Leslie McLemore is on the Executive Board of the Federation of State Humanities Councils. The President of that organization will be elected at its next national meeting. I have learned that Leslie is held in high esteem with the staff at the Federation, and you must push him for the next President of that organization.

No one knows better than I how hard the staff worked to present a state-wide conference, an Awards Banquet, and tolerate a Council meeting at the same time. They did a good job as always, and they deserve any pay increases that you can muster from your tight budget!

The silver tray is lovely. You were much too extravagant. I shall use it often with much gratitude to all of you.

I carry love for each of you in my heart, and I shall be around to continue admonishing you! However, I hope you'll take time to have a drink with me from time to time.

Sincerely,

Cora Norman

cc: MHC Staff
MHC Advisory Members
Dr. Edythe (Edie) Manza

A letter from my dear friend Aubrey Lucas follows.

THE UNIVERSITY OF SOUTHERN MISSISSIPPI

OFFICE OF THE PRESIDENT   **November 22, 1996**

**Dr. Cora G. Norman
5025 Wayneland Drive
Jackson, Mississippi 39211**

Dear Cora:

I am so very disappointed to learn that the dinner honoring you conflicts with a longstanding engagement here in Hattiesburg. Ella and I send our sincere regrets that we will not be on hand to tell you personally how much we treasure your friendship.

Cora, there is no one in Mississippi who has done more than you to take the humanities out to the people of our state. You have taken intellectual stimulation to places which were hungry for it. The programs of the Council have done what learning ought to do, and that is "to comfort the afflicted and to afflict the comfortable."

Among your many accomplishments is the way you have intentionally made the Council and thereby its programs more inclusive in terms of race, sex, age, political affiliation, geography, and economic background, and you have pushed this wonderfully diverse group into leadership positions throughout the state. We see a lot of "leadership programs" scattered about our state, but the "Cora Norman" program is one of our most effective.

We at The University of Southern Mississippi are deeply indebted to you for all you have done to assist us through the years, and we send to you our thanks for your friendship and our best wishes for much well-deserved happiness in the years ahead.

Yours very sincerely,

**Aubrey K. Lucas
President**

AKL/jbt

xc: **Dr. Barbara Carpenter**

Box 5001 • Hattiesburg, Mississippi • 39406-5001

A "Tribute to Cora Norman," from the Mississippi Institute of Arts and Letters, prepared by Aubrey Lucas and presented at their June 9, 2007, awards dinner.

A TRIBUTE TO CORA NORMAN
MISSISSIPPI INSTITUTE OF ARTS AND LETTERS
GREENWOOD, MISSISSIPPI
JUNE 9, 2007
BY
AUBREY K. LUCAS

It is difficult to think of the Mississippi Institute of Arts and Letters without Cora Norman, who has supported the Institute from its beginning and has served on its Board of Governors and as its President. During her presidency last year, the Institute had one of its more successful and delightful annual dinners in Oxford.

Over twenty-four years Cora made profoundly significant contributions to our State as the Founding Executive Director of the Mississippi Committee on the Humanities which later, under her leadership, became the Mississippi Humanities Council.

Cora was also active in the League of Women Voters and urged women to register to vote and to run for public office as she did in 1990 when she ran for state auditor. She said on one occasion, "To get women to run for public office, we must mentor, we must collect public money for them and stick with them."

-2-

Following her retirement in 1996, she served as chair of the Rust

College Committee on Academic Relations, on the boards of the Mississippi

Musicians Hall of Fame and the Virginia Gildersleeve International Fund for

Women; chair of the International Visitors Center of Jackson; and president

of the Jackson League of Women Voters. She received a Fulbright-Hayes

Seminar scholarship to attend a five-week women's studies workshop in

China. And she contributed greatly to a successful campaign to create a

Mississippi Commission on the Status of Women. She took her own advice

which she had given to others in retirement, "Forget age, and set some

worthwhile goals."

In 1977 the Mississippi Humanities Council inaugurated the Cora

Norman Lecture Series in honor of Cora, and the lecturer in 2006, Dr.

Marjorie Julian Spruill, formerly of The University of Southern Mississippi

and now the University of South Carolina, paid this tribute to Cora.

-3-

It is a great pleasure to return to Mississippi. And to have the opportunity to return to present a lecture TO an institution I admire - the Mississippi Humanities Council - in HONOR of another Mississippi institution I greatly admire-Dr. Cora Norman....

I owe a great debt to Cora Norman as an important role model in my formative years-from 1981 through to the present and into the future! She is today a great example of how to live life fully and happily afer retirement-continuing to make major contributions here in her home state and jet setting around the world, continuing to learn about and enjoy other cultures.

...Cora Norman has always provided an example of woman's achievement and leadership as well as the ability to bridge the gap between academia and the "real world," to bring scholarly research and theories to bear on current issues, helping us resolve the problems we face today with

-4-

more wisdom and humanity. ...Cora has brought people

together, black and white, rich and poor, urban and rural,

women and men-to talk about IDEAS and VALUES and

BOOKS and the ARTS, and helped us learn and grow. And

she made us think-and think TOGETHER-saying to

Mississippi-as did the title of one great Mississippi

Humanities Council series- "Mississippi, Let's Talk About

it." Thank you Cora for all of these things.

Tonight the Mississippi Institute of Arts and Letters says "Thanks"

to Cora Norman for helping to make the MIAL an important organization

in the promotion of Arts and Letters in our State.

APPENDIX B: THE CORA NORMAN LECTURE SERIES

Leslie Burl McLemore and the council members of 1996 authorized the Cora Norman Lecture Series; I remain indebted. Dr. Peggy Prenshaw presented the inaugural lecture in 1997 in conjunction with the Mississippi Humanities Council's 25th Anniversary Celebration in Jackson. I was so pleased that Peggy agreed to give the lecture because we worked side by side for so many humanities programs through the years.

Dr. Samuel DuBois Cook, president emeritus of Dillard University, gave the second lecture, "Black-Jewish Relations: Where Do We Go from Here?" The American Association of University Women, Jackson; the League of Women Voters, Jackson; Museum of the Southern Jewish Experience; and 100 Black Men of Jackson co-sponsored the event in 1999.

Left to right: Samuel DeBois Cook, Gemma Beckley, and Gayle Leftwich.

The University of Mississippi hosted the third Cora Norman Lecture in the Humanities in 2001. Dr. Elliott West of the University of Arkansas lectured on "DeSoto Meets Jesse James: A Report from South and West." We thanked Chancellor Robert Khayat and Provost Carolyn Ellis Staton for their generous hospitality and support of the lecture and reception and thanked the faculty and staff of Ole Miss and the Center for the Study of Southern Culture for their assistance in making the occasion possible.

Mississippi University for Women in Columbus held the fourth Cora Norman Lecture in the Humanities in their Nissan Auditorium. Dr. Jeannie Whayne from the University of Arkansas spoke on "Chasing Hope in a 'Wild and Sickly Country': Two Families, Two Destinies in the Arkansas Delta" in 2004.

The War Memorial Building in Jackson in 2006 was the site of the fifth Cora Norman Lecture in the Humanities. Dr. Marjorie J. Spruill from the University of South Carolina gave the lecture, "Awake, Aware and Deeply Polarized: Mississippi Women and the International Women's Year Conference of 1977." Since I was the program chair for Mississippi's International Year program, I learned much from Dr. Spruill's research on the conservatives who took over the program.

Through the years, numerous donors supported the lectures, and I appreciated their contributions to the establishment of the series. Many of my friends made contributions, and again, I owe thanks to my mentor, Dr. Katharine Rea, for her efforts in raising financial support. I also know that Barbara Carpenter and Brenda Gray worked very hard to make all the necessary arrangements and to assure excellent programs.

All Mississippians are indebted to those persons who formed the charter membership of the Mississippi Humanities Council. They came together, and without any prior knowledge of each other, united to launch a new program in Mississippi that was available to all people of the state.

The charter members were:

Porter L. Fortune, Chair	Robert Mayo
John Bettersworth	Charles Moorman
Owen Cooper	Linwood Orange
J. O. Emmerich	Matthew Page
Thomas Flynn	John A. Peoples, Jr.
Jack Gunn	Sandra Powell
George Howell	Sarah Rouse
Betty DeVall King	Estus Smith
R. A. McLemore	Parham H. Williams, Jr.

Since I devoted much of my time to securing proposals for public humanities programs for the council to fund, I remain indebted to the project directors who received our first year's regrant monies. The project directors were not only innovative but also daring. Confrontation between different groups in a community was common, and the idea of actually inviting citizens to an open forum to discuss educational issues was indeed an alien one. Please note that there were only a few regrants made for programs south of Jackson. The following were project directors of the first year's programs:

George Abraham, Vicksburg

Margaret Walker Alexander, Jackson

Russell C. Baker, Jr., Philadelphia

Milton Baxter, Jackson

Mary Benjamin, Jackson

Jane Bryan, McComb

Tom Dulin, Winona

Norris Allen Edney, Lorman

Ms. James Estes, Oxford

Dorothy Fitts, Oxford

Matthew Fogarty, Carthage

Joanne Guyton, Hernando

Darlus Hall, Natchez

Tommy Hart, Greenville

Betty Hearne, Blue Mountain

Beverly Herring, Canton

Troy Holliday, Ripley

Lenora Hudson, Jackson

David C. Jones, Durant

Byrle Kynerd, Jackson

Woodley Lott, Perkinston

Ruby Lyells, Jackson

Ed Meeks, University

Mary Musgrove, Itta Bena

Ms. Brent Nickle, Oxford

Jeanette Phillips, University

Willie Price, University

Jack Shank, Meridian

LePoint Smith, Cleveland

Archie Strahan, Gautier

Clyde Strickland, Perkinston

Eleanor Walters, Cleveland

William Washburn, Blue Mountain

Harold T. White, Booneville

Ted Alexander	1984-1988
Ted Ammons	1994-1998
Kenneth W. Andrews	1987
Ben Bailey	1988-1992
Gemma Beckley	1994-2002
Mary Benjamin	1982-1986
John K. Bettersworth	1972-1977
Ed Bishop	1987-1991
Gerald Blessey	1985-1988
Imogene Borganelli	1978-1983
Lucie R. Bridgforth	1990-1994
Jane Bryan	1991-1996
J. O. Carson	1979-1980
Frances Coleman	1991-1995
Ed Collins	1977-1978
Owen Cooper	1972-1978
Rosia Crisler	1984-1989
Joan Cunningham	1982-1986
Ellis Woolfolk Darby	1993-1996
Barbara Dease	1994-1998
Ed Dolin	1977-1978
Juanita Doty	1996-1998
Charles Dunagin	1980-1984
David C. Dunbar	1992-1996
Celia Emmerich	1985-1989
J. O. Emmerich	1972-1977

Joseph L Fant	1988-1990
Thomas Flynn	1972-1976
Porter L. Fortune, Jr.	1972-1977
Velvelyn Foster	1988-1992
George Godwin	1974-1978
Sid Graves	1988-1992
John Guice	1980-1984
Jack Gunn	1972-1977
Michael Harrington	1995-2003
Constance Slaughter-Harvey	1977-1982
Robert Haubert, Jr.	1991-1992
William Haynie	1980-1984
Carey Hearn	1984-1989
Henry Hobbs	1984-1987
Barbara Holland	1992-1996
Troy Holliday	1994-2002
George Howell	1972-1981
Mary Hartwell Howorth	1980-1984
Roy Hudson	1978-1983
Linda Wilson Jackson	1991-1996
Newton James	1977-1980
Newton Ward James	1994-1998
Leslie Johnson	1980-1984
W. J. Johnson	1977-1982
Linda Kay	1989-1993
William C. Keady	1987-1989

Robert Khayat	1985-1988
Betty DuVall King	1972-1974
Harriet DeCell Kuykendall	1987-1991
Gregory Lane	1993-1996
Billie Lee	1997-2002
T. W. Lewis, III	1984-1992
Nelda Lott	1977-1980
Charles D. Lowery	1986-1991
Aubrey Lucas	1977-1980
Charles Lucht	1980
Jeanne Luckett	1990-1994
Darwin Maples	1977-1980
Robert Mayo	1972-1978
William T. McGehee	1983-1988
Leslie McLemore	1992-1999
R. A. McLemore	1972-1975
Paul McMullan	1977-1982
Charles McTeer	1978-1983
Charles Moorman	1972-1975
Alpha Morris	1992-2002
Jessie Mosley	1981-1984
Jessie Mosley	1994-1996
Luther Munford	1983-1988
Lewis Nobles	1992-1994
James Noonkester	1984-1988
Linwood Orange	1972-1977

Matthew Page	1972-1978
William Pennington	1975-1978
John A. Peoples, Jr.	1972-1978
Sarah Percy	1975-1978
John Peterson	1989-1992
Cindy Phillips	1995-2002
Evelyn Polk	1982-1988
Hazel Portwood	1978-1983
Sondra Powell	1972-1974
Peggy Prenshaw	1984-1991
Vivian Presley	1995-1999
Anna Quinn	1980-1984
Ardenia Rambeau	1988-1992
Katharine Rea	1984-1988
Clyda Rent	1990-1994
Madlyn Richard	1987-1989
Frank Riley	1981-1984
Dollye Robinson	1984-1988
Jack Rogers	1996-2003
Sarah Rouse	1972-1977
Nicholas Saikley	1987-1991
David Sansing	1978-1983
William Scaggs	1978-1981
Charles Sewell	1982-1986
Adib Shakir	1992
Miriam Simmons	1977-1980

Estus Smith	1972-1984
James Patrick Smith	1991-1996
Carolyn Ellis Staton	1988-1990
John Hampton Stennis	1996-2002
Patricia Stevens	1984-1987
Will Sullivan	1994-1998
Rowan Taylor	1991-1992
Billy Thames	1989-1993
Roy Thigpen	1978-1981
Cleopatra Thompson	1990-1992
Johnnie Tollison	1991-1996
Allye Faye Turner	1988-1992
James Wade	1984-1987
Robert Walker	1989-1993
Jerry Ward, Jr.	1984-1988
Walter Washington	1977-1980
Ila Wells	1976-1981
Ann White	1996-2002
Jack White	1994-1999
Sam White	1988-1992
Parham H. Williams, Jr.	1972-1977
Peyton Williams	1976-1981
Robert E. Wolverton	1982-1986
Kent Wyatt	1977-1982
Aurelia Young	1974-1977

Those professors who dared go into the rural communities of Mississippi in our early days of the public humanities program had many experiences and stories to share. I'm sure, with the intervening years, that I omitted some who were much involved, and I apologize for any person left off the following list. I should have kept a daily journal as David Sansing suggested when we launched the program.

Ann Abadie	Howard Carpenter
Dale Abadie	Kit Carter
George Abraham	Bill Cash
John Quincy Adams	A. Cavell
Margaret Walker Alexander	Luana Clayton
June Allen	George Cochran
Andrew Badger	Ancilla Coleman
Curtis Baham	Mary Coleman
Ben Bailey	Aaron Condon
Sarah Banks	Bill Cooley
Taunya Banks	George B. Crawford
Jack Bass	Rosia Crisler
Gemma Beckley	David Crosby
Mary Benjamin	Joan Cunningham
Robert E. Bergmark	Barbara Dease
David J. Bodenhamer, Jr.	Roy DeBerry
Lucie Bridgforth	Allen Dennis
Wes Busbee	James Downey
Price Caldwell	Bill Durrett
Clarice Campbell	Terry Everett

Tom Flynn

Don Fortenberry

E. C. Foster

Velvelyn Foster

Gary Fox

Kathy Gilbert

Margaret Gorove

Patricia Grierson

John Guice

Jack Gunn

Page Gutierrez

Shelton Hand

Vagn Hansen

Nancy Hargrove

Evans Harrington

Michael Harrington

Alferdteen Harrison

C. James Haug

Jan Hawks

Betty Hearn

Carey Hearn

Nell Henderson

Ginger Hitt

Ralph E. Hitt

Barbara Holland

Jo Hollman

Lou Holloway

Ellistine Holly

Roy Hudson

Clarence Hunter

Lizette Hurst

Robert Jenkins

Dick Johnson

Larry Johnson

Frances Karnes

Linda Kay

Arthur H. Kinnard, Jr.

Seena Kohn

Curt Lamar

David Landry

James Lea

Charles E. Lewis

T. W. Lewis, III

Barbara Longest

Frederick Lorenzo

Nelda Lott

Woodley Lott

Lil Lovette

Charles Lowery

Ronald G. Marquardt

Suzanne Marrs

John Marszalek

Ken McCarty

Robert McElvaine

Jesse McKee

Leslie Burl McLemore

David McMillan

Edward McMillan

Richard Middleton, III

George Mitchell

Michael Mitias

Lorene Morgan

Alpha Morris

Luther Munford

Wallace Murphree

Lawrence Nelson

Sylvester Oliver

Linwood Orange

Joe Parker

Bill Parrish

Randall Patterson

Mary Libby Payne

William Pennington

John Peterson

Ivory Phillips

Robert Phillips

Nell Pickett

Mabel Pittman

Noel Polk

Peggy Prenshaw

Virginia Quarles

Michael Queyja

Annie Quinn

Michael Rabalais

Bennie Reeves

Tom Richardson

Barbara Ricks

Dollye Robinson

Jack Rogers

Oscar Rogers

Sarah Rouse

Bill Russell

Maureen Ryan

Charles Sallis

David Sansing

Bill Scarborough

B. N. Shaw

Dorothy Shawhan

John Ray Skates

Constance Slaughter

Estus Smith

Robert Smith

Marjorie Spruill

Joe Stockwell

Gary A. Stringer

William Sullivan

Johnny Tolliver

Lucy Turnbull

Alec Valentine

Roosevelt Wade

Durr Walker

Robert Walker

Jerry W. Ward, Jr.

William Washburn

Glenn Watts

Ila Wells

Milton Wheeler

Jack White

O. F. White

Samuel L. White, Sr.

David Wicks

Martha Wilkins

Clyde Williams

Peyton Williams

Parham H. Williams, Jr.

Robert E. Wolverton

Forrest Wood, Jr.

Aurelia Young

MHC Sponsored Awards

1993   Peggy Whitman Prenshaw
      Humanities Scholar Award

      E. S. Bishop, Sr.
      [First] Public Humanities Achievement Award

1994   Alferdteen Harrison
      Humanities Scholar Award

      Governor William F. Winter
      Public Humanities Achievement Award

1995   Ben Bailey
      Humanities Scholar Award

      Katharine Rea
      Public Humanities Achievement Award

1996   Ginger Hitt
      Chair's Award for Special Achievements in the
      Humanities

      Robert Jenkins
      Humanities Scholar Award

      Billy Thames
      Public Humanities Achievement Award

1997   Carolyn Vance Smith
      Public Humanities Achievement Award

      James Patrick Smith
      Chair's Award for Special Achievements in the
      Humanities

      Jerry Ward, Jr.
      Humanities Scholar Award

1998   T. W. Lewis, III
      Public Humanities Achievement Award

1999   Randall Patterson
          Humanities Educator Award

2000   Libby Aydelott
          Public Humanities Achievement Award

          Elizabeth Sarcone
          Humanities Educator Award

2001   Ann Abadie
          Humanities Scholar Award

          Pamela Pridgen
          Public Humanities Achievement Award

2002   Lillie Lovette
          Humanities Educator Award

          Leslie Burl McLemore
          Humanities Educator Award

2003   Jack White
          Humanities Scholar Award

          Martha Swain
              Chair's Award for Special Achievements in the
              Humanities

          Ovid Vickers
              Chair's Award for Special Achievements in the
              Humanities

2004   B. N. Shaw
          Humanities Scholar Award

2005   Alpha Morris
          Public Humanities Achievement Award

          Robert Walker
          Humanities Scholar Award

2006   Michael Harrington
    Public Humanities Achievement Award
    Robert Jenkins
        Chair's Award for Special Achievements in the
        Humanities

2007   Dennis Mitchell
        Chair's Award for Special Achievements in the
        Humanities

OTHER AWARDS

1989   Rosia Crisler
        Teacher of the Year, Hinds Community College

2007   George Abraham
        Award for Literacy Excellence—Best Business
        Book of 2007, BooksandAuthors.Net